IN-LINE
SKATING

IN-LINE SKATING

FITNESS SPECTRUM SERIES

Suzanne Nollingham

Frank J. Fedel

Human Kinetics

Library of Congress Cataloging-in-Publication Data

Nottingham, Suzanne, 1958–
    Fitness in-line skating / Suzanne Nottingham, Frank Fedel.
       p. cm. -- (Fitness spectrum series)
    Includes bibliographical references and index.
    ISBN 0-87322-982-7
    1. In-line skating. 2. Physical fitness. I. Fedel, Frank, 1959– . II. Title.
  III. Series.
  GV859.73.N68 1997
    796.21--dc21
                                                   96-48336
                                                      CIP

ISBN: 0-87322-982-7 (pbk.)

Developmental Editor: Julie Rhoda; **Assistant Editor:** Sandra Merz Bott; **Editorial Assistants:** Jennifer Jeanne Hemphill and Amy Carnes; **Copyeditor:** Regina Wells; **Proofreader:** Bob Replinger; **Indexer:** Craig Brown; **Graphic Designer:** Keith Blomberg; **Graphic Artist:** Doug Burnett; **Photo Editor:** Boyd LaFoon; **Cover Designer:** Jack Davis; **Photographer (cover):** © Jane Dove Juneau; **Illustrators:** Doug Burnett and Studio 2-D

Human Kinetics books are available at special discounts for bulk purchase. Special editions or book excerpts can also be created to specification. For details, contact the Special Sales Manager at Human Kinetics.

Printed in Hong Kong by Paramount Printing 10 9 8 7 6 5 4 3 2 1

Human Kinetics
Web site: http://www.humankinetics.com/

United States: Human Kinetics, P.O. Box 5076, Champaign, IL 61825-5076
1-800-747-4457
e-mail: humank@hkusa.com

Canada: Human Kinetics, Box 24040, Windsor, ON N8Y 4Y9
1-800-465-7301 (in Canada only)
e-mail: humank@hkcanada.com

Europe: Human Kinetics, P.O. Box IW14, Leeds LS16 6TR, United Kingdom
(44) 1132 781708
e-mail: humank@hkeurope.com

Australia: Human Kinetics, 57A Price Avenue, Lower Mitcham, South Australia 5062
(08) 277 1555
e-mail: humank@hkaustralia.com

New Zealand: Human Kinetics, P.O. Box 105-231, Auckland 1
(09) 523 3462
e-mail: humank@hknewz.com

Contents

PART I

PREPARING TO IN-LINE SKATE

In-line skating is the nation's fastest growing recreational activity. In a span of less than 10 years, in-line skating has grown from virtual obscurity to one of the top 20 participation sports in the United States. And with basic information about technique and equipment, in-line skating is almost as simple as walking. It's a lifestyle fitness activity for anyone, from athletes to amateurs and from kids to grandparents.

People have many reasons for in-line skating. Some people skate train for heavy competition; some use in-line skating as cross-training for skiing, cycling, and water sports; others skate because the lateral leg motion complements traditional fore/aft movements such as running. Most people, however, skate for one simple reason: It's fun. Other than a minimal investment for skates and protective gear, it's free. You can skate just about anywhere that you can find smooth, dry pavement.

For people who need a way to modify their fitness regimen to include only activities that put minimal stress on the joints, ligaments, and tendons, in-line skating can be the answer. Its fluid, graceful movement patterns offer a significant muscular workout and cardiovascular challenge yet don't leave you sore and aching. Whether your goals include weight loss, athletic training, or simply cruising, in-line skating is easy to learn and provides the option for a nonimpact cardiovascular workout.

Part I of this book provides all the information you need to begin in-line skating for fitness. The first chapter explores the varied benefits of in-line skating for those who are less active and searching for the perfect fitness activity, those who are looking for new activities to spice up their current exercise routines, and those interested in expanding fitness levels to compete or just skate hard for general fitness.

Chapter 2 covers all you need to know about making the right equipment choices to match your in-line skating goals. For example, you'll learn about which components and attributes are the most important when selecting an in-line skate. Braking systems and how they affect the cost of your skates are explained, as is how the type of surface on which you'll be skating dictates the size and durometer of the wheels you select. Finally, learn what protective gear and apparel are necessary for safety and how to maintain equipment for optimal performance.

Chapter 3 provides self tests to assess your readiness to skate train, which will help you decide in which training zone or program you should begin. You'll learn a practical way to test your current fitness level—the skating fitness test (a time trial). This test can be performed at any point in your training program.

Chapter 4 includes everything you'll need to know about skating safely, including the "Rules of the Road," traffic laws, and tips for skating in groups, in bike lanes, and on bike paths. You'll also be introduced to some of the basic skills necessary to get you started striding, turning, and stopping on your skates.

Chapter 5 highlights the necessity of warm-up and cool-down periods in order to avoid muscle fatigue, strain, and injury. We'll also suggest some practical warm-up and cool-down exercises, as well as skate-specific stretches.

No excuses! If you haven't tried in-line skating yet, you're in for an exhilarating experience. Now, get ready to roll because in-line skating is one of the most effective ways to get and stay in shape!

In-Line Skating for Fitness

Although in-line skating is a relatively new sport, having made it's initial surge in popularity around 1989, already several different segments of participants have developed. Among them are dancers, hockey players, racers, recreational/fitness skaters, and aggressive skaters. Everywhere you look, it seems that more and more people are cruising around on skates: college students who use skating as an inexpensive method of transportation, "30-somethings" who want to remain active without overspending on equipment, teenagers who want a "cool" form of exercise and want to compete in roller hockey, and older adults who want to enjoy some of the fun that this new sport has to offer.

Aggressive skaters perform "rail slides," "curb grinds," and other inspired maneuvers. Speed skaters try to go faster and faster, always seeking a more aerodynamic skating position and better technique. Most people skate for fun and recreation. Recreational in-line skating is an exciting activity and is relatively easy to master. Couple these attributes with the fact that it provides a reasonably inexpensive recreational, fitness, and social channel, and you can appreciate how in-line skating can easily become a part of people's daily lives. While in-line skating may seem to be geared toward the younger sports participant, its low-impact nature holds much appeal for older exercisers, too. No matter what the age, skill, or fitness level, everyone can reap the health benefits of in-line skating.

Why In-Line Skate?

Because in-line skating provides the most important components of a good all-around fitness program—cardiovascular or cardiorespiratory fitness (endurance), muscular fitness (muscular strength and muscular endurance), body composition, and flexibility—you'll be able to actually see and feel the benefits. For instance, your resting heart rate will typically be lower when your fitness level is increased. Your good cholesterol (HDL-cholesterol) level may increase, you'll have a reduced amount of body fat, and you'll have more energy.

You'll also be able to complete normal daily tasks more easily, and you'll sleep better afterward. All of this because you strap on a pair of skates and have some fun. Sounds like a pretty good deal!

Aside from the gains in fitness, in-line skating provides two added benefits: balance and coordination. Whether you decide to use in-line skates to train hard or just to improve your general fitness, the balance and coordination you acquire simply by participating will improve your overall body balance and coordination in everyday movements.

If part of your focus is on calorie burning and body fat management, consider that by skating at a comfortable pace three to five days per week for 30 to 45 minutes each day, you can burn calories at a rate similar to other modes of exercise such as cycling and jogging. A 30-minute skate session typically burns 300 calories or more, depending on your equipment, the surface on which you skate, your body weight, wind conditions, and the terrain (hills or flat pavement). The rate of calorie burning is directly related to your body weight; thus, at the same intensity, a 130-pound female will burn fewer calories than her 160-pound male counterpart. Also, shorter in-line skate frames, smaller-diameter wheels, head winds, hills, and rougher surfaces all add to the number of calories you expend in an in-line skating session.

Moreover, in addition to burning calories, you'll tone your leg muscles—especially the front and back of the thighs, the buttocks, and the inner thighs—due to the unique fore/aft and lateral motion of the in-line skate stroke.

In-line skating also offers variety in workouts, such as LSD (long, slow distance), time trialing (skating a distance for time), intervals (alternating higher-intensity skating periods with active-rest periods during which you skate at a lower intensity), sprints, and drafting behind someone. All of these training techniques can be done no matter what your fitness level; if your level is only average, you simply won't skate as fast or as long as someone with a higher fitness level. By varying your training techniques, you can make progress in speed, endurance, and skill without fatiguing quickly. As your fitness level increases, you'll increase your speed and ability to skate longer.

More serious fitness enthusiasts turn to in-line skating for intense workouts without the resultant muscle soreness experienced by participation in more ballistic sports such as basketball and running. The workout intensity that in-line skating can provide is so good that even the U.S. Olympic ice speed-skating team uses in-line skates as a method of off-ice training.

In-line skating doesn't need to be taken to the extremes of high-speed training; recreational skating not only provides many benefits but also is convenient. Compared with four of the top five participation sports in the United States in 1994 (walking, swimming, bicycling, and indoor exercising), in-line skating ranks as a very convenient activity in terms of equipment necessary, initial fitness level requirements, diversity of benefits, and the potential to socialize during performance (see fig. 1.1). Since virtually anyone can participate, it's an ideal once-a-week activity that everyone can enjoy, along with other sports activities. You can make your in-line skating workouts "family fun times" when the whole family gets out for a bit of recreation, fresh air, and exercise!

Benefits of In-Line Skating

The fitness benefits offered by in-line skating are adequate to provide you with the amount of daily physical activity recommended by sports medicine experts. Since one important prerequisite for health is a moderate amount of physical activity performed most days of the week, in-line skating fits well into a healthy lifestyle. Becoming a regular in-line skater can help you develop cardiovascular fitness and reduce your body fat, as well as improve muscle toning, strength, and endurance, all of which are related to good health. The results you achieve will be based in large part on what level of participation you choose: easy, moderate, or intense.

Cardiovascular Fitness

Cardiovascular fitness (also known as cardiorespiratory fitness or aerobic fitness) is a measure of the body's ability to do work (exercise). As you exercise, the heart pumps blood to the working muscles. This blood has been oxygenated by the lungs. The working muscles use some of this oxygen and send the deoxygenated blood back to the lungs for reoxygenation. As your fitness level increases, your muscles are able to utilize more oxygen, which in turn increases the amount of work you can perform. This is reflected in your aerobic fitness level; the higher your fitness level, the more work you're able to do. As your fitness level and work capacity increase, you can train longer or faster, which will typically help improve your efficiency at performing an activity. And so the upward spiral of fitness and ability to work goes; with cardiovascular fitness you can do more, and if you do more, you get improved aerobic fitness. For participants interested in high-level performance, this combination of cardiovascular fitness and muscular efficiency provides a much greater opportunity to perform at advanced levels for a longer time before experiencing fatigue.

In-line skating offers tremendous potential to enhance your aerobic fitness level. It yields the same cardiovascular benefits of high-impact sports such as jogging, racquetball, and basketball without the undue stresses to the joints and muscular system. If your goal is to improve your fitness level, depending on your current level and rate of participation you can achieve gains of 10 to 30 percent in less than three months.

The heart rate response (how fast the heart beats in response to an activity) to in-line skating is compatible with the American College of Sports Medicine's recommendations for developing cardiorespiratory fitness. For a given level of work, the heart rate response during skating may be higher than during other activities. This is an important point to keep in mind if you're training for fitness. To achieve a similar calorie-burning (oxygen consumption) effect, you may need to keep your heart rate approximately 5 to 10 percent higher during in-line skating than during other sports such as running. This shouldn't be difficult, however; studies have demonstrated that skaters' perceptions of intensity appear to be based on calorie-burning intensity rather than on the heart rate.

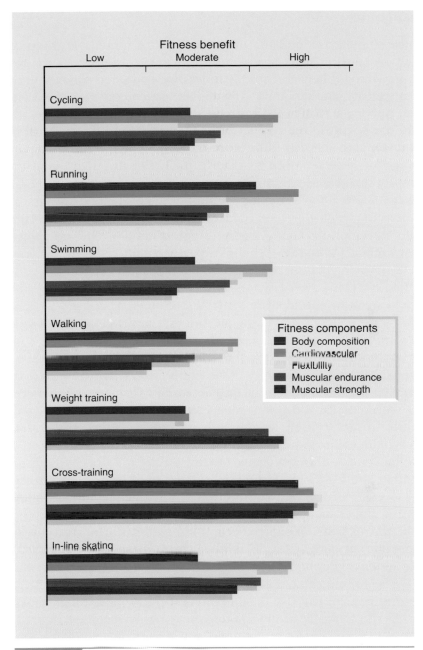

Figure 1.1 Fitness activities.

Muscular Strength

Muscular strength is a measure of the ability of a muscle or group of muscles to perform work against a significant resistance. As we get older, our strength declines steadily unless we engage in some type of physical activity. The repetitive, low-impact movements of in-line skating can provide sufficient leg exercise to maintain muscular strength. While it's not unusual to experience muscle soreness after a high-impact activity such as jogging or running, with in-line skating that type of muscle soreness isn't a problem, due mainly to its low-impact nature. In addition, the unique bent-knee position used during the glide phase forces the legs to support all of the body weight in a position in which they don't typically support much weight. This increases strength through a greater range of motion than do sports such as cycling and running. The increased strength you gain not only helps your skating but can cross over to other sports as well.

At first, you may become concerned that your leg strength isn't sufficient to allow you to skate for long distances. That's not a problem; just take it slowly and easily for the first few weeks. And if you need some encouragement, remember that one of the benefits of in-line skating is firm legs. Look at the legs of any in-line speed skater, and you'll see that the results can be impressive. Although you may experience muscle tiredness or fatigue sooner than an experienced skater, with practice and persistence you'll quickly develop muscular strength. In fact, muscle strength is one of the most noticeable impacts of an in-line skating training program.

The movement during a classic skating stroke not only extends or straightens the leg, as in walking or cycling, but also pushes the leg to the outside of the body, abducting the leg at the hip. This leg abduction and ensuing leg adduction, or returning the leg toward the middle of the body, use muscles not recruited during the linear (straight-line) activities of walking or cycling. These muscles, located on the inner thigh and on the gluteal region (see fig. 1.2), become stronger as a result of skating. The strengthening both assists in skating and minimizes the risk of injury when performing other activities, since those muscles will be less likely to be overworked.

Muscular Endurance

Muscular endurance is the ability of a muscle or group of muscles to repetitively perform a task without experiencing undue fatigue. In-line skating has a great potential for developing muscular endurance. Due to the unique biomechanics of the sport, the quadriceps muscles of the thighs remain contracted for an extended period during each stroke cycle. When a skater initially sets his or her foot down, the quadriceps of that leg must remain contracted throughout the entire glide phase of the stroke in order to support the skater. As the skater moves toward the push-off phase of the stroke, the quadriceps and gluteal muscles contract in coordination, producing forward propulsion. Immediately after push-off, the other leg is placed under the body for support, keeping the quadriceps muscles working for a large portion of the entire stroke cycle. This constant workload makes it necessary for the leg muscles to develop endurance. Increasing the duration of your skate workouts will enhance your muscular endurance.

© Ray Manning/Fedel Performance, Inc.

The muscular strength in-line skating builds is apparent.

	Aerobics	Cycling	Running	Swimming	In-line skating
Quadriceps	■	■	■		■
Hamstrings	■	■	■		■
Ankle			■		■
Hip extensors (buttocks)	■	■	■	■	■
Hip flexors	■	■	■	■	■

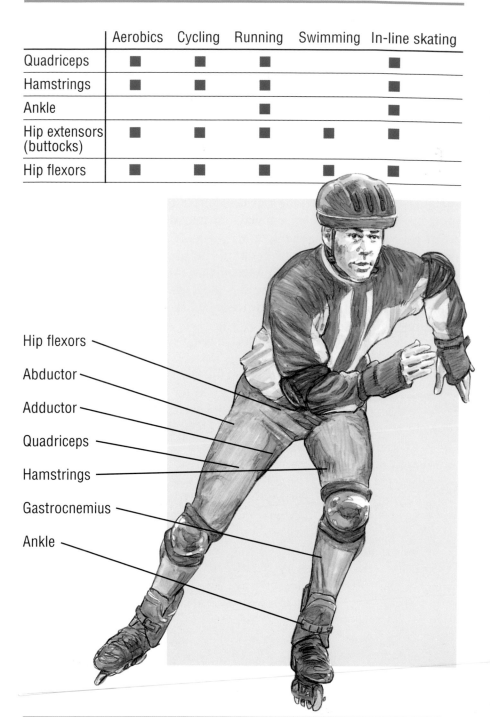

Hip flexors
Abductor
Adductor
Quadriceps
Hamstrings
Gastrocnemius
Ankle

Figure 1.2 Lower-body muscle groups used while participating in in-line skating.

Body Composition

Body weight alone is not an indicator of fitness level or health; the composition of the body (fat mass and lean mass) is just as important—or even more important—in many people. Fat mass, as the name implies, is simply the amount of the body that is composed of fat, while lean, or fat-free mass, is the balance of the body weight and includes such components as muscle, bone, organs, body fluids, and other tissue. Although some body fat is essential for normal body processes (storage of vitamins, protection of the internal organs, etc.), too much fat is related to many diseases, including heart disease, high blood pressure, and diabetes. An excess of body fat is also a detriment to mobility; people with too much body fat are doing more work than is necessary by carrying extra weight.

The range of body fat percentages that is considered healthy varies by gender. For men, it is generally 13 to 20 percent of total body weight; for women it is 18 to 25 percent. Note that the healthy range does not begin with 0 percent, so some body fat obviously is essential for good health. Still, that healthy amount is typically less than the amount carried by the average sedentary, nonexercising individual. For example, if a man who exercises regularly weighs 200 pounds and has 15 percent body fat, he has 30 pounds of total body fat. If another 200-pound man has body fat of 25 percent, he is carrying 50 pounds of fat—66 percent more excess baggage!

In determining the ability of any activity to help you control the amount of body fat you are carrying, remember that the number of calories burned during the activity is directly related to the amount of fat you can burn. In general, for every pound of body fat you wish to burn, you need to expend 3,500 calories. Therefore, if one activity allows you to burn considerably more calories than another activity, it will burn fat faster than the other as well. But before you get excited and look for an activity that burns the most calories, be forewarned: the more calories you are burning per minute, the more work your body is doing. This simply means that in order to maximize your calorie expenditure, you will need to work harder (regardless of which activity you're doing).

Also, you won't necessarily be burning only fat when you expend calories; you can also be burning carbohydrate or protein. Generally, lower-intensity exercises get a larger percentage of their calorie burning from fats, while higher-intensity exercises get a larger percentage from carbohydrates. The trade-off may be that if you perform lower-intensity exercises exclusively, you'll need to spend much more time to achieve the same calorie-burning effect of doing a higher-intensity exercise.

There is no "best activity" for burning calories; your ability to burn calories will depend almost exclusively on your fitness level. In order to burn 20 calories per minute (a very high intensity), you'll need to perform work at twice the intensity as when you burn 10 calories per minute. Of course, some activities are more fun and are perceived as being easier than others compared with the effort you expend. While typically those activities are extolled as being the best for burning fat, when you come right down to it, you can burn fat only as fast as your fitness level will allow you to burn fat.

One of the greatest benefits of in-line skating is that it's an enjoyable, nonstressful form of exercise. In fact, many former sedentary individuals who regularly engage in in-line skating as a form of recreation will skate for two hours or more without feeling that they're really exerting themselves. So, while you're out there skating around and having a good time, you're also making progress toward reducing body fat or maintaining a healthy level.

The number of calories you burn during in-line skating will vary considerably; table 1.1 gives some average calorie-per-minute values for an average 150-pound male and 130-pound female. If your body weight is higher or lower, your calorie-burning effect will be proportionally reduced or increased. Also, if you use racing skates (five-wheel or four-wheel with longer frames), your calorie burning at each speed will be lower; you don't need to expend as much energy while skating with them. This may be due to the greater gliding distance you can typically achieve with longer skate frames—you are able to "rest" for a longer period of time with longer frames.

Flexibility

Flexibility, the degree to which joints can be put through a range of motion, can be enhanced through in-line skating. This is a real benefit, as loss of flexibility can lead to inability to perform activities easily or properly, injury, or pain on movement. The distinctive lateral leg action of in-line skating requires a certain degree of flexibility of the inner thigh muscles, so as you improve your technique, and balance, your inner thigh muscles will be stretched farther during each stroke. Since proper skating position requires the knees to be bent significantly, the functional range of motion of the knee joint is also exercised.

Table 1.1 Caloric Expenditure During In-Line Skating					
Skating Speed		Calories burned			
MPH	KPH	Male Per min.	Female Per min.	Male 30 min.	Female 30 min.
8	12.9	7.4	6.4	223	193
9	14.5	8.9	7.7	268	232
10	16.1	10.4	9.0	313	271
11	17.7	11.9	10.3	358	310
12	19.3	13.4	11.6	403	349
13	20.9	14.9	12.9	448	388
14	22.5	16.4	14.2	493	427
15	24.1	17.9	15.5	538	466

© Jane Dove Juneau

Flexibility allows you a fuller range of motion during your stroke.

However, while the increases in range of motion (flexibility) gained from in-line skating alone are noticeable, optimal flexibility requires additional attention to stretching. Therefore, stretching exercises are recommended for skaters, to minimize the stiffness sometimes associated with beginning an exercise routine.

Coordination

Coordination is a broad term that includes the ability to perform an action without using extraneous movement. A coordinated action uses the minimal amount of muscular energy and the minimal amount of unnecessary movement needed to perform that action. When watching an individual who is skilled at a particular sport, you can usually ascertain which movements are coordinated—they look almost effortless. An example is a tennis player hitting a forehand volley versus a backhand; the forehand volley usually looks much easier—it's a more coordinated movement. "Balance-in-motion" sports such as skiing, cycling, waterskiing, and ice-skating all require a certain degree of coordination to perform well. Likewise, the "dynamic balancing act" that takes place when you in-line skate is a multiple-joint, multiple-muscle, coordinated action. Because of this, it's imperative that you have coordination in order to perform it safely and gracefully.

For example, during in-line skating if you move your center of mass too far forward or backward, or if you lean to one side or the other beyond a certain point, you'll fall. But, just like with riding a bicycle, once the skill is mastered it becomes second nature. And the skills that you develop—balance, timing, coordinated movement, pacing, and others—will remain with you for the rest of your life. These are just a few of the reasons why many runners, skiers, cyclists, triathletes, and volleyball players use in-line skating to complement their sport-specific training.

A Sport for Competitors

For the hard-core exerciser who is looking toward racing, in-line skating will provide as much of a challenge as you desire. Whether you're interested in seeing how your best 10K time fares in comparison with the world record of 13:51 in the paced 10 kilometer (or 6.2 miles), which was set by Nate "The Skate" DiPalma on July 13, 1995, or planning to enter the famed Athens-to-Atlanta 85-mile Road

Skating Marathon held each October in Athens, Georgia, in-line skating is ready to test your mettle.

In this sport, you can experience a sense of accomplishment by improving your speed, your endurance, or your skills; skating either for speed (27 miles per hour was the average of "The Skate" during his 10K world-record-setting time trial) or for distance (entering a 50K or 100K race) will provide you with a rush. And once you've been able to compare your current performance with your previous performances, you'll find that competing against yourself can be a great motivator. Of course, the conventional method of competing against others is also challenging and exciting, and since many races incorporate age group rankings, you can see how you perform relative to others who are your age.

© John Laptad/F-Stock

Personal motivation to push your limit is often the best way to go the distance.

2

Getting Equipped

In this chapter, we'll cover everything from head to toe: from what to look for in a helmet to what type of socks to wear. The first section, which deals with selecting skates, focuses on your personal goals and what type of skate will work best for you. Next we'll discuss selection and proper use of protective gear (including a helmet), followed by tips on how to keep your skates in top working condition. Then we'll spend some time on how to dress for various weather conditions.

Selecting In-Line Skates

Before you rush off to the nearest store and buy your first pair of skates, you'll need to determine which components of a skate will be the most beneficial for your particular set of circumstances. Unfortunately, there is not a simple answer such as, "The XYZ skate is the best fitness skate on the market." Your level of interest, your budget, and your desire to have a functional and stylish-looking skate will all play a part in determining which skates best suit your needs. Since literally dozens of models are available, and you can spend anywhere from $40 to $500, and even more (some racers spend in excess of $1,000 on their skates).

When you take into consideration the style, performance components, and name associated with a skate, there is a strong association between how much you pay and what you get. For a new pair of comfortable, useful in-line skates, plan on spending a minimum of $170. With protective gear and a helmet, you can walk out of the store ready to skate for around $300. You always have the option of purchasing a used pair of skates (for children whose feet are constantly growing, this is a reasonable option), but for adults and older teenagers, new skates are usually more desirable.

In many sports, equipment is not a significant advantage. However, with in-line skate racing, equipment can provide a definite edge in terms of speed and performance. Longer frames and larger wheels make the biggest difference by far. Most five-wheel skates have longer frames, which allow you to glide longer and help you travel farther with each stride. A few specially designed four-wheel skates (with longer frames) are also available for racing and stability at high speeds. If you're using typical four-wheel skates designed for recreational use, remember they aren't made to go quite as fast as racing skates and therefore won't perform as well as racing skates, will take more effort, and won't feel as stable.

If you're considering racing skates, here are a few tips.

- Off-the-shelf racing skates (as opposed to racing boots and frames purchased separately) usually are equipped with either a removable brake or no brake at all; they're your least expensive racing skate option.
- Be aware that plastic boots are typically much larger and require additional hardware when compared to leather boots, so they can weigh significantly more. This additional weight is one reason why many racers choose to custom build their skates with lightweight boots and frames.
- For racing, you'll want larger, lighter-weight wheels.
- When skating indoors, wheels should be of higher durometer (80A and above; more information on durometer appears in the Wheels section later in this chapter). For skating outdoors, wheels with a durometer of as low as 75 to 78A are used.
- Racing skates are generally not recommended for casual skating or beginning racers; the longer frames typically found on these skates don't allow you to turn easily, and they're difficult to use if you're just learning to skate.

What should you look for in your first pair of in-line skates? Several components can have a noticeable effect on a skate's performance. Basic skate components include the boot and closures (lace/buckles), frame, bearings, brakes, and wheels.

Boots

The shell, or boot, of most recreational in-line skates can be made of a number of materials with plastic being the most common, followed by leather and fabric. The material used is not the major consideration in terms of a skate's performance; however, proper design of the boot is critical. There are a few considerations in terms of boot design.

A major consideration for anyone just getting involved with in-line skating is the degree of ankle support provided by the boots. Look for boots with cuffs that are high enough to completely cover your ankle bones. Most recreational models fall into this category (see fig. 2.1). Perhaps the most critical aspect of ankle support is the lateral (side-to-side) support that can help make skating more fun and less tiring for your lower legs. An easy way to examine the ankle support before you try a boot on is to hold it in one hand and squeeze the cuff together. Then, try bending the cuff from side to side. If it flexes easily, it may not have adequate support for you.

Once you're comfortable with the amount of ankle support, make sure the liner (inside of the boot) is comfortable as well. The inner surface of the liner should be soft enough to minimize friction against your leg; if the liner is too coarse, you may wind up with raw spots on your ankles from the constant movement of your leg against the liner while skating.

When you are trying on new boots, be sensitive to any pressure in the toe area, arch, top of the foot, or heel. If any discomfort in these areas occurs, ask a knowledgeable salesperson how you can remedy the situation before you buy the skates. For example, if your heel is moving from side to side too much, you may need to go to another brand or model to get adequate heel support in the boot.

Laces or Buckles?

The fastening system used on in-line skates varies from manufacturer to manufacturer and from model to model. The two basic types are laces and buckles. While buckles provide the convenience of simply putting your foot into the boot and clamping three buckles, laces

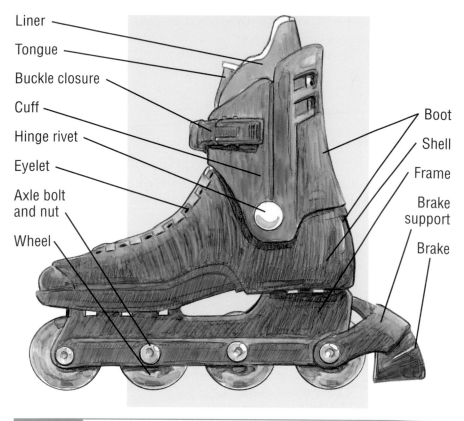

Liner

Tongue

Buckle closure

Cuff

Hinge rivet

Eyelet

Axle bolt and nut

Wheel

Boot

Shell

Frame

Brake support

Brake

Figure 2.1 Components of a four-wheel in-line skate.

offer the fine-tuning aspect of boot fit. You can tighten laces at spots on your boots that buckles won't. For most people, it's a matter of which feels better and will better suit their needs.

Frames

Experienced skaters should invest in a high-performance skate model, something with a long frame (at least 10 inches from front axle to rear axle). Fitness skaters who skate several times a week should look for a midrange four-wheeled skate with supportive boots. Occasional skaters should purchase a four-wheeled skate, which is the best all-around skate for fitness and cross-training. Some manufacturers make three-wheeled skates for smaller feet, but four-wheeled models typically offer more stability as well as a longer wheelbase than three-wheeled skates.

The length of the frame on the skates you purchase will largely determine their responsiveness. Longer frames (beyond 12½" and up to 14½") typically available only for racing skates, come with five wheels, are better suited to long, straight skating courses at higher speeds. Shorter frames are more maneuverable, but they don't offer as much stability at higher speeds. This is especially unsettling when you are skating downhill.

Material used in the frames is another important consideration. While steel frames are the most durable, aluminum and synthetic frames offer lighter weight as well as shock absorption. Also, the composition of synthetic frames differs with the model; you'll need to "test drive" the skates you're considering to see how the frames feel.

A four-wheel skate is recommended for most in-line skating activities.

Bearings

Bearings are one of the two major components that can make a big difference in the performance of the skate; older, dirty bearings are slow and noisy. Bearings also are the sole component on in-line skates that are rated. The Annular Bearing Engineers Committee (ABEC) sets worldwide standards for precision bearing manufacture and tolerance. ABEC ratings for skate bearings are 1, 3, and 5 (though the ratings do go higher, the higher levels aren't used for in-line skating). Although the higher the rating, the higher the bearing's precision (and price), the ABEC rating does not imply anything about the quality of the components used for the bearing or its suitability for a particular application. Many top-level skaters have used good quality, ABEC 1-rated bearings successfully for years. Even so, skating with bearings that have a non-ABEC rating (sometimes known as "semiprecision") is usually noticeably noisier than skating with ABEC-rated bearings, and the lower-quality bearings don't tend to last as long. Value-priced skates typically don't have ABEC-rated bearings. Some midpriced skates come equipped with ABEC 1- or 3-rated bearings, while almost all bearings on high-end skates are ABEC 1 or 3.

Braking Systems

You have several braking systems from which to choose, including the standard, passive-system heel brake which works great with a little instruction on how to use it. Among newer braking systems are Rollerblade's Active Brake Technology® (ABT), which is activated simply by pressuring the rear ankle cuff that in turn activates the brake while allowing the skater to keep all eight wheels on the ground; Oxygen's Power Braking System® (PBS), which has a spring load that forces the brake down to the rear wheel; the Ultra-Wheels Disc Braking System® (DBS), which uses both a hard urethane, wheel-shaped brake that is slowed by friction and spacers that provide pressure to the interior of the brake; and the Seneca Sports toe brake, reminiscent of the old roller skate toe brake. Which works best? The answer is that they all do a fairly good job if you spend some time practicing how to use them. Although beginners might find it easier to learn stopping with one or more of the many newer braking systems available, racers don't even use brakes; they employ a T-stop (see chapter 4).

Wheels

Wheels are the second components (aside from bearings) that can make a tremendous difference in the performance of an in-line skate. Wheels come in a variety of standards and are characterized by the following design features.

- **Diameter:** The height of the wheel, or the outside diameter, measured in millimeters (mm). Most recreational skates are equipped with wheels of 72 to 76 mm in diameter.
- **Durometer:** The hardness or firmness of the wheel, rated on the Shore A scale (a "hardness" measurement rating—there is also a Shore D scale that is used for other applications). Softer wheels have lower ratings (75A), while harder wheels have higher ratings (93A).
- **Profile:** The shape of the wheel when viewed from the front or rear.
- **Compound:** The composition of the urethane used in making the tread, or surface materials of the wheel.
- **Core:** The center portion of the wheel, also known as the hub. The core is surrounded by the urethane tread and the center of the core provides a "seat" for the bearings.

Diameter. Typical recreational skates have wheels ranging from 72 to 76 mm in diameter, racing skates are equipped with wheels of 76 to 80 mm in diameter, and children's skates usually come standard with 60 to 70 mm wheels. Aggressive skaters use wheels as small as 47 mm.

Wheel size has perhaps the largest noticeable effect on wheel performance. For maneuverability, quick turning, quick accelerations, and control, smaller (70 to 72 mm) wheels are preferred; that's why aggressive skaters use them. Wheels with a somewhat larger diameter (76 mm) are typically used for recreational skating due to their ability to roll farther and more easily than wheels with a smaller diameter. However, their increased size diminishes their ability to turn as quickly—they have a tendency to want to travel in a straight line—as well as making them a bit harder to accelerate.

Durometer. Selection of durometer is usually made on the basis of several factors, including body weight, surface, need for traction, and shock absorption preference. Generally, heavier people use higher-durometer wheels; a 200-pound man may get almost the same performance characteristics with an 85A-durometer wheel that a 120-pound woman gets with a 78A-durometer wheel.

Skating surface plays a part in the need for traction as well; higher-durometer wheels don't usually provide good traction on rougher surfaces such as pebbled pavement or very porous asphalt; therefore lower-durometer wheels are commonly used on these surfaces. Shock absorption is another personal preference consideration: lower-durometer wheels tend to have better shock absorption qualities and provide a better ride, since they are softer.

The downside to lower-durometer wheels is that they have a shorter life in terms of how long they last before becoming excessively worn; higher-durometer wheels tend to last longer.

Profile. The various profiles available can be grouped into a few main categories as shown in table 2.1.

A wheel with a blunt, almost flat profile performs better for the rapid maneuvers of an aggressive skater, while a more rounded profile allows for significant traction, control, and reduced rolling resistance needed by hockey players. Moderately pointed recreational wheel profiles offer a lower rolling resistance than in-line hockey wheels for a smoother ride, a larger contact area than racing wheels for more control, and a larger diameter than aggressive wheels for longer gliding.

The very pointed racing wheel profile is not necessary for most recreational skaters; aside from the fact that some recreational skates won't fit the typically larger diameter (76 to 80 mm) of racing wheels, the larger ground contact of most recreational wheels allows for better control.

Compound. The compound used in the manufacture of various wheels affects the rebound of the wheel, or the degree to which it returns energy rather than absorbing it. Most skaters agree that the wheels made with high-rebound urethane feel "lively," whereas wheels made with low-rebound urethane are "unresponsive."

Core. To satisfy the ever-developing technical appetite of in-line hockey players, in-line racers, and fitness skaters, manufacturers have attempted to improve on the basic concept of the wheel by modifying the design of the core. Special "vibration-dampening" cores, "airflow" cores, and "ultrastiff" cores are available for specific purposes. Most cores are made of plastic, but newer aluminum cores (which allegedly provide more efficient energy transfer and increased stiffness) are also an option.

Table 2.1
Categories of Wheel Profiles

Profile description	Ground contact area	Rolling resistance*	Users
Blunt, almost flat	Very large	High	Aggressive
Shallow, rounded	Large	Moderate	Hockey
Moderately pointed	Moderate	Moderate	Recreational
Very pointed	Very small	Low	Racing

*Rolling resistance is based also on durometer and diameter of the wheel.

Getting the Proper Fit

Once you've determined the proper skates for your needs, you'll want to make sure they work right for you. Here are some tips for buying skates and obtaining a proper fit. (Follow these guidelines when looking for a used pair, too.)

- **Check the durability of the frame.** Hold the skate, wheels up, between your legs, grab each end of the frame with both hands, and twist. The frame should be sturdy enough to with stand the torque without deforming or twisting.
- **Check the bearings.** Good bearings will turn smoothly and quietly when you spin the wheels. If you hear a scratching or grinding noise, or if you see the wheels rotate slowly or wobble, you're probably not looking at skates that will endure much skating.
- **Check the wheels.** Inspect to see that the wheels are the appropriate durometer, size, and profile for your skating goals.

If the skates pass all of the preliminary tests, you can test them for proper fit and function:

- Put the skates on in the store to see how they fit. One of the biggest mistakes novice skaters make is to assume that because the skates are the same size as their shoes, they'll be a perfect fit. Some skates are as much as a full size larger than they are size-rated. In addition, since feet come in all sorts of distinct shapes and sizes, manufacturers have a difficult time making a skate that will provide a snug fit for everyone; you might need to try on several brands before you find skates that fit you properly.

- When you try on a skate, you should be wearing the same socks you will use when you're skating. Proper socks for in-line skating are important for comfort, performance, and injury prevention (see the end of this chapter).
- Sit on a chair and kick the heel of your skate against the ground, feeling your foot move backward into the boot. Do this on both boots, then stand up and see how much room you have left in the skate. If your foot position changes after you kick your heel against the back of the boot, tie or buckle the boots again to a comfortably snug fit, and see how they feel.
- Skates should fit snugly on your feet, and you should feel no significant movement by your foot forward or backward, side to side, or up and down in the liner of the boot. Liners have a tendency to compress with use, so you don't want to purchase an already loose skate. Extra movement of your foot in the liner can cause blisters, calluses, and irritating hot spots due to excessive repetitive movement. On the other hand, the skates should not fit so tightly that they cut off circulation or produce pain or

© Ray Manning

Clockwise from left:"Turbo Core," removable aluminum core, larger diameter racing core, and solid "aggressive" core.

pressure spots. If you feel uncomfortable pressure anywhere on your feet while trying on skates in the store, be forewarned: the pressure will only get worse when you're out skating. You shouldn't expect skates with plastic boots to break in and conform to your feet; the plastic doesn't change shape. Find skates that fit properly right out of the box. Just as important as your foot being securely contained in the liner of the boot, the liner shouldn't move significantly inside the boot once the skates are laced or buckled. Excessive movement of the liner in the boot can lead to loss of control and even injury while you're skating.

- Make sure that you get into a skating position while trying out the skates. Get into a partially crouched pose, with knees and ankles flexed. If you feel pressure on the top of your foot or ankle when you bend forward at the ankle, you need to try another pair. Also, when you're standing upright, your toes should touch the end of the boot; when you get into a crouched skating position, they should come back slightly. If possible, try skating for a short distance. If the cuffs of the boots bend sideways too easily, you should move on to another pair with a more rigid and supportive cuff. Likewise, if the boots are too binding, look for a more forgiving boot, or loosen the buckles or laces at the top of the cuff.

- Check to make sure you're comfortable with the braking system. Skate for a short distance and see how the braking system responds. Remember, when you need to stop, you want to have a brake that is easy to use and works well.

If you find a pair of skates that passes all of the tests, you're ready to roll. It's also a good idea to buy protective gear at the same time that you purchase your skates. You may be able to get a discount on a package—helmet, wrist guards, knee and elbow pads, and padded shorts. Even if you can't get a special deal, making all your purchases at once is a good way to ensure that you'll have the protection you want when you first put your skates on.

Maintaining Your Skates

After you've purchased your skates, you'll need to know how to take care of them so they'll last a long time. Some basic guidelines can save you money and make your skates work better.

- **Skate maintenance:** For keeping your boots clean, you can use a simple household cleaner and water to wipe down the outside and inside of plastic boots. The liners can be kept clean by occasionally removing them and letting them "breathe." When the liners are removed, clean the inside of the boots.

- **Wheel maintenance:** Rotating your wheels, or making sure they wear evenly, is as important for your in-line skates. By skating on the same set of wheels without rotating them occasionally, you will wear down the inside edges of the wheels. Wheels with worn edges can make skating a less comfortable, almost uncontrollable experience.

  Not only does wheel rotation improve your ability to skate effectively, but it also saves you from replacing your wheels prematurely. Wheels that are rotated properly are designed to last for about 300 to 400 miles (for an average 150-pound skater); if not properly rotated, they can last for only 150 miles or less. That means that you can double or almost triple the life of the wheels if you take care of them properly! Take a few minutes to rotate your wheels every now and then, when you notice that they're becoming worn.

  To rotate your wheels, simply use a skate tool to remove the axle bolts, wheel, axle, and bearings. Then, the simplest way to proceed is to swap the first and third wheels, and the second and fourth wheels on typical four-wheel in-line skates. For a five-wheel skate, you have a few choices: the easiest are to put the wheels in reverse order (front wheel to rear position, second wheel to fourth position, and leave third wheel in place), or move all wheels forward one position and put the front wheel in the rear position. After every second rotation, change wheels from one skate to the other, making sure the inside of the wheel gets placed into the other skate as the outside of a wheel.

- **Bearing maintenance:** The easiest and most productive way to maintain your bearings is to plan ahead: don't skate in areas with a lot of dust, dirt, or water. It's difficult if not impossible to keep a set of bearings working properly once they've been exposed to water. If your bearings become dirty, your first step in keeping them operational is to wipe the outside surface with a clean, dry rag (don't use oil; it attracts dirt). If they sound gritty when you spin them, they can be either cleaned (contact your local skate shop to ask about this) or replaced.

- **Brake maintenance:** While you can't do anything to increase the life of your brake pad, you can make sure it is functional each time you skate. Make sure you check the condition of your brake before you put your skates on. If the brake is worn to the point where it is not allowing you to stop effectively, you can get a replacement brake pad from a skate shop.

Gearing Up for Safety and Comfort

Depending on the in-line activity you choose, you may consider a variety of protective gear. For example, if you'd like to learn to ride the half-pipe like the aggressive skaters do, you'll need thicker, heavy-duty knee pads (ask your local retailer to show you various types) and padded pants.

Helmet

Other than your skates, the helmet is your most important purchase. Although the risk of injury while in-line skating is small compared with many other sports, the risk is still present. You should make it a rule to keep your helmet with your skates; that way you'll always have it handy when you want to go skating.

Be sure the helmet you purchase is ASTM, ANSI, or Snell approved. These certifications are made by organizations that test helmets and certify only those that meet strict safety guidelines. Most bicycle helmets meet these certification requirements, but you should check to be sure; your head is worth the few extra moments it takes.

Verify that the helmet you select is the right size and is adjusted properly. It should not have room to move around on your head; the fit should be almost snug. Some helmets have sizing pads that allow for small adjustments, but the initial fit should be very close. When you put the helmet on, adjust the ear straps on both sides so that the joining of the front and rear of each strap occurs just beneath the bottom of the ear.

Elbow, Wrist, and Knee Protection

It doesn't matter which aspect of in-line skating you'll be focusing on—fitness, racing, aggressive skating, or hockey—wrist, knee, and elbow pads that slip over your limbs and are fastened by straps will provide you with better protection than those that just lie on top of your clothing and strap around your arms and legs. Although wrist protection may not eliminate the risk of fractures, it can have a dramatic effect in protecting your arms, wrists, and hands from injury if you fall.

Most elite racers don't use elbow or knee pads. For these highly experienced skaters, protective gear restricts movements somewhat, as well as increases wind resistance. Of course, you probably won't be skating at 25 miles per hour as they do, so the minimal added wind resistance of protective gear is not an issue. In summary, despite the fact that some people find protective gear to be restrictive, you'll have a much better chance of remaining injury free if you wear the gear, and we suggest you do!

Padded Shorts

As a beginner, you might consider using padded skate shorts, also useful for playing hockey, riding the half-pipe, or skating steep downhills. Again, ask your local retailer which shorts they recommend; as long as there is protection surrounding the hips and tailbone, the major difference among products may be only the cost.

Socks

Many skaters complain of blisters, a problem that can result from wearing the wrong socks. Thor-lo® makes socks especially for in-line skaters. These socks are designed without ribs, which can cause pressure points on your feet. They also don't bunch up to cause blisters.

© Jane Dove Juneau

Drink water before, during, and after your in-line skating workouts.

Insoles and Footbeds

Sensations along the soles of your feet send instructions to your brain regarding which adjustments you need to make for better balance. Explore the benefits of purchasing custom insoles/footbeds for enhanced performance and improved balance.

Dressing for the Weather

Although many types of clothing are available for every weather condition, during warm weather all you need are some comfortable shorts and a top, whatever allows freedom of movement and is comfortable. Elite racers choose skintight Lycra® or spandex suits, which cut down on wind resistance (and look impressive).

In colder weather, many in-line skaters continue to traverse the city streets, wearing the latest climate-appropriate clothing. If you are considering skating in colder weather, you need to be aware of the effect of too much, as well as not enough, clothing on your body. If you wear lots of heavy clothing, thinking that it will keep you warm, you may become overheated. In colder weather, you should put on only enough clothing to keep you comfortable yet dry. As you exercise, you perspire; if your clothing is not made of materials that allow that perspiration to evaporate, you'll get wet, which can lead to your becoming uncomfortable and cold.

Plenty of new fabrics are available that allow you to exercise comfortably in a temperature range of 30 to 40 degrees Fahrenheit. The key to using these fabrics is to keep your skin dry—don't wear cotton against your skin; as you sweat the cotton becomes saturated, and your body will feel the cold faster through wet cloth than through dry cloth. Polypropylene or other synthetic fabrics are the materials of choice for use against your skin when exercising. Wind-breaking fabrics should be used as an outside layer to allow perspiration through to the atmosphere while keeping the cold wind away from your skin.

Adding Up the Costs

Assuming you are just getting involved in the sport and don't already have any equipment, let's take a look at some of the costs associated with in-line skating. The two scenarios we'll examine are Low Budget (equipment you'll need if you want to use in-line skating for fitness) and High Budget (if you're more serious about the sport and are considering using it as your main fitness activity).

The term low budget does not refer to the quality of the equipment; it implies being very cost conscious. As we explained earlier, purchasing low-quality, low-cost equipment will not only make your skating experience suboptimal, it will also cost you more in the long run since you will need to upgrade to good components in order to achieve even fair performance. The low-budget figures include all of the basic equipment you'll need to become a safe skater during the warm-weather months.

The high-budget plan includes most of the equipment used by a serious in-line fitness enthusiast. This would be a person who skates whenever the weather permits, does his or her own general maintenance (replacing wheels, bearings, etc.) and wants to enjoy in-line skating to its fullest.

Selecting equipment outlined in the low-budget plan has already been discussed. For the high-budget plan, you'll need to know what to look for in terms of a skate carrying bag, skate tools, a skate computer, footbeds, sports eyewear, and a heart rate monitor.

A well-designed in-line skate bag will be able to comfortably hold your skates and have extra room for some basic tools (outlined below), as well as a towel, water bottle, and any other skate accessories. It should be padded well enough to protect your car seats from getting ripped by your skate tools or any sharp objects in your skate bag, as well as being comfortable to carry (with a shoulder strap or handle).

A variety of in-line skate tools are available. Based on the brand of in-line skate you purchase, make sure the tool you select has the proper size allen wrench(es) to fit your skates.

While there are only a few in-line skate computers available, they provide you with information on your skating speed and distance skated. Because in-line skate wheels come in a number of different diameters, you must enter the correct wheel size into these skate computers in order to get accurate results. Look for a skate computer that is easy to mount onto your skate and has a display that is large enough to be easily read while it is mounted on your skate and you're standing up.

When looking for insoles or footbeds for your in-line skates, make sure the pair you select will fit into your boots. Some in-line boots have unusual shapes and may not accommodate an insole or footbed.

In terms of selecting good sports eyewear, keep in mind that any type of eyewear will protect your eyes from wind and debris (a bug in the eye is painful!). The most desirable eyewear is functional; the lens extends farther around the face rather than just covering your eyes. Most sport sunglasses have interchangeable lenses for different light conditions. In bright sunlight, wear a darker lens; in overcast or cloudy conditions an amber or yellow lens is preferable.

Purchasing a good portable heart rate monitor will be critical if you will be using information about your heart rate responses to skating to monitor your training. A good heart rate monitor will include a transmitter (which picks up the electrical signals of your heart beating) that is held against your chest by an elastic strap, and a wireless receiver/display that you wear on your wrist. The display will provide a readout of your heart rate (we'll discuss heart rate training zones in part II). Other models also allow you to select an audio alarm which will sound if you exceed your training heart rate zone. These features can be beneficial if you want to keep a detailed log of your workouts, or if you want audible feedback, to warn you when your heart rate exceeds a certain rate.

Getting What You Pay For

In addition to using less than optimal materials and components, inexpensive skates don't usually have high-rebound urethane wheels and precision bearings. We recommend investing in mid-to high-end skates; they work well and also have resale value. Of course, if you have already purchased lower-priced skates, you still have the option to upgrade your components.

ADDING UP THE COSTS

LOW BUDGET		
SKATES	$	180
PROTECTIVE GEAR		
PADS, WRIST GUARDS		35
PADDED SHORTS		35
HELMET		70
TOTAL	$	320
HIGH BUDGET		
SKATES	$	375
PROTECTIVE GEAR		
PADS		40
HELMET		70
WRIST GUARDS		25
PADDED SHORTS		35
SKATE CARRYING BAG		50
SKATE TOOLS		20
SKATE COMPUTER		50
COLD WEATHER SUIT		150
INSOLES/FOOTBEDS		70
SPORTS EYEWEAR		70-150
HEART RATE MONITOR		100-150
TOTAL	$	1,055-1,185

3

Checking Your In-Line Skating Fitness

Because in-line skating places demands on your cardiovascular system, an important precaution is to assess your readiness to begin training. Most healthy adults will have no problem beginning an exercise program if they approach it in a sensible manner. However, a small number of individuals may have a health profile that warrants additional information before engaging in such a program.

Test Your Health and Fitness

The following questionnaire is designed to help identify individuals for whom a physician's visit is advisable before beginning an exercise program, and to classify individuals with respect to their current activity level.

Answer all questions honestly; it's for your own benefit. Scoring is explained at the end of the test. If the result is a bit disappointing, don't worry. You'll have plenty of time (the rest of your life!) to get on track using the programs we outline in this book. So, get out a pen (and if you don't want to write in this book, some paper). Let's see where your starting line is; we'll talk about your finish line later.

ASSESSING YOUR IN-LINE SKATING FITNESS

Cardiovascular Health

Check the description that best applies to your cardiovascular condition. This is a critical safety check before you enter any vigorous activity. (Note: If you have a history of heart disease or circulatory problems, start the in-line skating programs in this book only after receiving clearance from your doctor—and then only with close supervision of a fitness instructor.)

No history of heart disease or circulatory problems	____(3)
Past ailments have been treated successfully	____(2)
Such problems exist, but no treatment required	____(1)
Under medical care for cardiovascular disease	____(0)

Injuries

Check the description that best applies to your current injuries. This is a test of your musculoskeletal readiness to start an in-line skating program. Warning: If your injury is temporary, wait until it is cured before starting the program. If it is chronic, adjust the program to fit your limitations.

No current injury problems	____(3)
Some pain in activity, but not limited by the injury	____(2)
Level of activity is limited by the injury	____(1)
Unable to do much strenuous training	____(0)

Illnesses

Check the description that best applies to your current illnesses. Certain temporary or chronic conditions can delay or disrupt your in-line skating program. (See warning under "Injuries.")

No current illness problems	____(3)
Some problem in activity, but not limited by it	____(2)
Level of activity is limited by the illness	____(1)
Unable to do much strenuous training	____(0)

(continued)

Age

Check the age group that applies to you. In general, the younger you are, the less time you've spent slipping out of shape.

Age 20 or younger	____(3)
Age 21 to 29	____(2)
Age 30 to 39	____(1)
Age 40 or older	____(0)

Weight

Check the description that best represents how close you are to your own definition of ideal weight. Excess fat is a major indicator of unfitness, but it is also possible to be significantly underweight.

At or very near ideal body weight	____(3)
Less than 10 pounds above or below the ideal	____(2)
10 to 19 pounds above or below the ideal	____(1)
20 or more pounds above or below the ideal	____(0)

Resting Pulse Rate

Check the description that best applies to your current pulse rate on waking up in the morning but before getting out of bed. A well-trained heart beats more slowly and efficiently than one that's unfit.

Below 60 beats per minute	____(3)
60 to 69 beats per minute	____(2)
70 to 79 beats per minute	____(1)
80 or more beats per minute	____(0)

Smoking

Check the description that best applies to your smoking history and current habit (if any). Smoking is the number-one enemy of health and fitness.

Never a smoker	____(3)
Once a smoker, but quit	____(2)
An occasional, light smoker now	____(1)
A regular, heavy smoker now	____(0)

(continued)

In-Line Skating Background

Check the description that best applies to your experience with in-line skating. Where you start with an exercise program is determined largely by your current level of exercise. This is especially important for skill-related sports such as in-line skating.

Have some experience with in-line skating	_____(3)
Roller-skated or ice-skated within the last one to two years	_____(2)
Roller-skated or ice-skated more than two years ago	_____(1)
Never in-line skated, roller-skated, or ice-skated	_____(0)

Recent In-Line Skating

Check the description that best applies to your most recent in-line skating experience (within the past month). Recent participation in an activity typically reflects a person's ability to perform an activity, as well as his or her fitness level.

In-line skated for more than 30 minutes continuously	_____(3)
In-line skated for at least 15 minutes continuously or 30 minutes intermittently	_____(2)
In-line skated for less than 15 minutes, either continuously or intermittently	_____(1)
Haven't in-line skated	_____(0)

Related Activities

Check the description that best applies to your usual participation in other continuous-motion, aerobic activities (running, bicycling, cross-country skiing, racewalking, rowing, stair climbing). The cardiovascular endurance acquired through cross-training with other aerobic activities allows you to do more work with less fatigue.

Regularly practice continuous aerobic activity	_____(3)
Sometimes practice continuous aerobic activity	_____(2)
Engage in nonaerobic activities	_____(1)
Not regularly active	_____(0)
Total Score	_____

A score of 20 points or more represents high overall health and fitness. You should have no problem doing any of the beginner-level (green zone) workouts lasting less than 30 minutes, as well as most of the blue zone workouts.

A score of 10 to 19 points places you in the average category for overall health and fitness. You should be able to complete the beginner-level (green zone) workouts, but you may need to do them at the lower end of the suggested intensity level to reduce fatigue.

A total of less than 10 points is considered a low overall health and fitness score. If you have the determination to stick with it, in-line skating is an ideal activity to help you bring your score up! By beginning a prudent program of exercise with in-line skating, you can impact your body weight, your resting pulse rate, and your activity level.

No matter how high or low your overall score, if you scored a 0 on either the cardiovascular health or the injuries question (questions 1 and 2), you should check with your doctor before beginning your training program.

Test Your Skating Fitness

It's always a good idea to check with your physician before beginning any exercise program. If your last complete physical took place more than a year ago, it's time to schedule an other appointment. Once you've been cleared by your physician to engage in an exercise program, you can take the next step: doing an in-line skate test such as the one that follows to estimate your cardiovascular fitness level.

This test is a three-mile time trial. A time trial is an event that challenges your ability to get from the start to the finish in the least time possible. No drafting behind other skaters or any vehicles (including bicycles) is allowed; it's you against the clock. The object here is to get a good idea of how fast you can skate this course in conditions that will be reproducible throughout your training program. If unusually high winds, high temperatures, or traffic are present, you can still do this test, but the results won't be an accurate representation of your ability to sustain a high speed over a three-mile course.

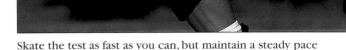

© Andy Anderson/F-Stock

Skate the test as fast as you can, but maintain a steady pace

What You'll Need

- **A course.** Lay out a three-mile course on a smooth, traffic-free surface. A one-way course (starting in one place and finishing somewhere else) is preferable, but if you need to skate laps to get three miles, that's OK too. If you need to put in a turn, make sure it's not a 180-degree turn in a small area; make it a broad turn, so that you don't need to decrease your speed significantly to negotiate it.
- **Your skates.** Make sure they're in proper operating condition—brake not worn down, all bolts tightened.
- **Protective gear.** This includes a helmet, wrist guards, knee and elbow pads, and padded shorts if you're a beginner.
- **A stopwatch.** You can substitute a regular wristwatch, but it's easier to have a timer with an automatic start and stop so you don't need to remember what time you started and when you finished.
- **Proper clothing.** Based on the temperature, humidity, and wind conditions, select clothing that will allow you to remain comfortable throughout the trial (see chapter 2).

The Test

1. Don't eat anything for at least one and a half to two hours before your test.
2. Immediately before performing the test, make sure you're adequately warmed up (five minutes of easy skating should do the job).
3. Make sure your timer is set to start when you're ready.
4. Skate the three-mile course as fast as you can while maintaining a steady pace. Don't be discouraged if you need to slow down or stop; pick up the pace when you can, and continue until you finish.
5. Record the total time it took you from when you started until you reached the finish line. Consult table 3.1 or 3.2 to see where you rank in the fitness category classifications.

Table 3.1
Males

Fitness classification	Three-mile time-trial time*
Below average	More than 14 minutes
Moderate	11 to 14 minutes
High	Less than 11 minutes

*Subtract 2 minutes from these times if using racing or five-wheel skates.

Table 3.2
Females

Fitness classification	Three-mile time-trial time*
Below average	More than 17 minutes
Moderate	13 to 17 minutes
High	Less than 13 minutes

*Subtract 2 minutes from these times if using racing or five-wheel skates.

Retesting and Checking Your Progress

You can do this test once per month to check your progress. Keep track of your results in your training journal (refer to chapter 15). At first, you may notice large improvements in your performance. As you get faster, the change in your improvement will become smaller, but don't worry—this is a natural occurrence.

4

In-Line Skating the Right Way

Next in the progression of your goal of fitness in-line skating is learning all of the right things to do once you're geared up and ready to go. In this chapter we'll discuss safety guidelines and what techniques are necessary to skate effectively and efficiently. We'll also give you some tips on how to improve your striding technique, and we'll profile some of the best places to skate.

Skating Safety

One of the most important aspects of skating is safety. You've purchased your skates and you want to get rolling, but before you take that first stride, it's a good idea to know something about skating safety on the road. The International In-line Skating Association (IISA) has developed and promotes a set of guidelines called "Rules of the Road." A summary of the rules follows, along with our own added recommendations.

1. **Skate smart.** Always wear protective gear—helmet, wrist guards, knee and elbow pads. Master the basics—moving, stopping, and turning.
2. **Skate alert.** Control your speed. Watch for road hazards. Avoid water, oil, and sand. Avoid heavy traffic.
3. **Skate legal.** Obey all traffic regulations. When on skates, you have the same obligations as any other operator of a wheeled vehicle.
4. **Skate polite.** Skate on the right, pass on the left. Announce your intentions by saying "passing on your left." Always yield to pedestrians. Be a goodwill ambassador for in-line skating.

Here are a few suggestions we'd like to add:

- Anticipate the need to slow down or stop. Do not skate in traffic unless you are comfortable with and can use your heel brake effectively.
- Do not use headphones; it makes hearing traffic behind or around you difficult.
- Be courteous to motorists and cyclists; try to avoid making sudden and unexpected movements.
- Use hand signals to cue traffic, cyclists, and other skaters of your intentions. Left turn: Put your left arm straight out, pointing left. Right turn: Point your left arm straight up. Stopping: Point your left arm straight down.

    We don't recommend relying exclusively on this type of communcation when dealing with motorists. In addition to using hand signals, be sure motorists understand your intentions; try to establish eye contact, and be courteous—let them go first.
- When skating with friends, the lead skater should orally cue others of nearby traffic by saying "car up"; skaters in the back should cue those in front by saying "car back."
- Take lessons from an IISA-certified instructor. You can locate an instructor by checking with a local in-line retailer, a health club, parks and recreation, or by locating the general IISA Instructor Certification Program home page on the Internet at http://www.iisa.org/icp/ or by calling the program at 910/762-7004. They have an international "instructor locator" and can provide you with a list of qualified instructors in your area.
- Consider using a glove-mounted or glasses-mounted rear view mirror to keep you informed of traffic behind you while you're skating.

These suggestions will make skating a much more enjoyable proposition for everyone—from the skaters to the operators of vehicles with whom we share the road to the pedestrians on bike paths and walking tracks. When possible, consider skating in a group. Larger groups are more visible to other traffic, including vehicles pulling out of driveways or crossing at intersections.

Where to Skate

Some of the best places to practice your in-line skating skills are large store or church parking lots, high school or college tracks, playgrounds, parks, boardwalks, community centers, and industrial parks. (Be sure to ask for permission before entering a parking lot; it could save you some trouble.) Once you're comfortable and in control on skates, consider venturing out onto lightly traveled roads and bike lanes, as well as bike paths and paved walkways.

© Nagel Photo

Where you choose to skate offers as much enjoyment as skating itself.

Always pay special attention to the surfaces on which you'll be skating; cracked, gravel-covered, or uneven surfaces are not as safe or as fun as a flat, well-paved surface free of debris, oil, water, and sand. Even leaves and other small obstacles can be a hazard while you're skating if you're not aware of them. Pebbles can become launchpads for unsuspecting skaters; if you're in an area with debris on the skating surface, stagger your feet for stability until you can get to a site more suitable. Also, if you are in an area where black tar is used to fill the joints in the road, be aware that when the weather gets hot, the tar becomes sticky, and skating over it is difficult. If you encounter hot tar, you may get an unwelcome surprise as your wheels are stopped almost immediately when they try to roll across it.

Don't think you're limited to clearly paved streets on which to train or practice, however. Most roller rinks across the country now welcome in-line skating (as long as you don't have skates with exposed hardware that can damage their floors). In addition, a few cities offer skating indoors on the concourse of their football stadiums or athletic arenas. At the Pontiac Silverdome in Pontiac, Michigan, for example, skaters are allowed to use the smooth concrete indoor concourse for skating during the winter months.

When you get involved with the workouts in chapters 6 through 11, you'll want to have a location that will allow you to skate unencumbered by a significant amount of traffic, traffic lights, side streets, cross traffic, or pedestrians. Until then, you can enjoy skating almost anywhere that the ground is relatively smoothly paved and free of debris.

Skating Technique

Gaining fitness with in-line skating can be a pleasant experience, but once you've made some progress on your cardiovascular fitness, you can be held back from further progress if you don't learn proper skating technique. Technique is important for considerations of both safety (incorrect technique can lead to accidents or injuries) and practicality (if you're not skating properly, you're probably working harder than necessary or unable to work to your desired level of intensity).

Learning the basic skills of in-line skating—standing, striding, stopping, and turning—equips you to try just about all of the workouts in this book. After you've tried the basics, don't rush to become involved with advanced techniques. Go slowly. It takes a while to become proficient. Feel free to try all of the following skill progressions, in the order they are listed, to better set yourself up for success.

Start on a high-friction surface such as carpet or grass before braving the pavement. And remember, we highly recommend you play it smart with full protective gear—helmet, wrist guards, and knee and elbow pads!

Standing

For a beginner, the first function of in-line skating is to learn to stand properly on your skates. You'll do this to facilitate balancing techniques, as in-line skating is a balance sport. To adopt a secure, comfortable stance (refer to this as your "ready position") simply stand upright with both feet facing forward. Your feet should be hips' width apart. Make sure your knees and ankles are slightly flexed, without unnecessary tension in your legs. Arms and hands should be in front of your body; you should be able to see both hands peripherally while looking ahead.

An important fact to keep in mind is that if your hands and arms move back behind your waist, you're more likely to fall. So, take mental note of where they are at all times. To maintain optimum control, you should be aware of, and guard against, making unnecessary upper-body movements. Keeping the arms and hands in front also allows you to center your balance on the whole foot, with emphasis toward the balls of the feet instead of on the heels (which can also cause you to fall backward). Just as you instinctively know not to lean backward, never lean forward. Simply adjusting your arms and hands in front and standing upright will help you to move forward to the balls of your feet.

Striding

A typical in-line skating stride has distinct phases. To stride efficiently, you use a "support" foot/leg for balancing and gliding, and an "action" foot/leg for stroking (or pushing off). During each stride, the action leg pushes powerfully in a sideways motion as you balance and glide on the support side. The action leg then comes back under the hips to become the support leg—instructors call this regrouping.

While you are learning, your strides might resemble short, choppy steps. To remedy this, and to get into a more efficient skating position, start by angling both feet outward (kind of like a duckwalk) to feel pressure on the insides of the arches and on the balls of the feet. A realistic goal for striding is to be able to glide on the support leg/foot for longer and longer periods. At this stage in your technique, don't be too concerned about using your hands and arms to gain momentum. Their sole purpose at first is to help you balance, so remember to keep them in front of your body. Concentrate on relying on the movements of your feet and legs to propel you forward; use your arms only to help make slight corrections in movement if your legs and feet aren't getting you where you want to go.

If you pay attention, you'll notice that at first, your feet wander farther and farther apart during your stride. Try to focus on regrouping. With practice, striding will begin to feel more natural . . . more and more like walking. Following are some tips for improving your stride. Be sure to also master stopping and turning skills to get the most out of your workouts.

© Nagel Photo

Experiment with the timing of your striding movements to help you develop smooth, coordinated movements that will enhance your ability to skate easy or hard.

- Flex the front support leg at the knee and ankle to balance and glide. Think "chest over knee over ankle."
- Fully extend the action leg to get maximum power in your push-off.
- Balance your hips over your support foot; aim your hips in the desired direction of travel.
- Look ahead in the desired direction; keep your head and chin up.
- Add opposing arm movement for momentum once you're comfortable with your basic stride technique. Your arm swings should complement your forward movement by driving force fore and aft, not side to side.
- Stride with a full range of motion, constantly thinking about balancing with your hips closer to the ground during both the glide and pushing phases. This lowers your center of gravity.
- Bring your action leg back in after each push-off to regroup under your hips; this leg then becomes your support leg.
- Once you're comfortable with the foregoing tips, learn to push off by first leaning slightly on the outside edges of your wheels and rolling the ankle all the way to the inside edges (this is a more advanced technique).
- After pushing off the inside edge, continue your stroke to extend (and relax or loosen up) your ankle. As you bring this foot back under your hips to become the new support foot, this "relaxation" facilitates better balance along the sole of the foot.
- Focus on directing your push-off foot sideways, not backward.

Stopping

Stopping is another obviously useful skill. The beginner stop is performed using the standard "fixed" heel brake. This is the brake that is applied when you gently raise the toe of the skate with the brake attachment (usually the right skate). To initiate this action, you need to keep a few things in mind:

1. Begin in a ready position as explained earlier, with knees and ankles slightly flexed and arms in front of your body.
2. Keep an upright posture at all times!
3. Slowly move the braking foot (or action leg) forward, shifting your weight to your support foot (nonbrake leg) for balance.
4. Slowly lift the toe of the braking foot, while continuing to balance your weight on the support foot.

5. Gradually apply more pressure to the braking foot until you come to a complete stop. Do this by gently lowering your center of gravity (hips) over the support.

6. Keep in mind that it takes several feet to actually stop. Practice braking several times, and don't venture onto hills until you're comfortable stopping in a relatively short distance. To brake on steep hills start in a tall posture. Only after you've performed all of the other steps listed here, leverage the brake by sitting down slightly on the left leg. Another good drill is to practice braking in a straight line to prepare for skating downhill.

© David Roth

Practice coming to a complete stop so you'll have the skill when you really need it.

A T-stop is an alternative method of stopping. It is used by those who either do not have a heel brake (usually elite racers, hockey players, and aggressive skaters). To accomplish a T-stop follow these steps:

- As you coast forward, move one foot in front of the other.
- Next, turn the rear foot perpendicular to the line of travel behind the front heel. All the wheels on this back skate drag on the pavement, creating friction to help you slow down. When applying pressure on your back skate, be sure you don't put too much pressure on the back foot quickly; most of your weight will remain on your front foot. Note that the foot placement to accomplish this type of stop resembles a capital T; hence the name "T-stop."

Turning

After you get your strides down fairly well, you're ready to learn the basics of turning. Turning is not a simple task, but rather is the result of the coordinated and dynamic consolidation of much information, such as pressure application, body position, and skate direction. Turning can be done in a few different ways:

- **The A-frame turn:** This turn is started with a wide stance and is executed by slowly placing the weight on the outside skate (the skate on the outside of the desired turn) on its inside edge. As you shift weight to the outside leg, your body will begin to turn in the direction that the outside skate is facing. One note of caution: this turn is not effective in high-speed situations; it is a basic move that allows for development of balance and coordination.
- **The parallel turn:** This turn uses both skates simultaneously to initiate the turn. Coasting forward with feet parallel, stagger the inside foot toward the direction of the new turn. Slowly edge both skates in the same direction, while keeping ankles and knees flexed. This turn is useful for higher-speed skating and works well on flats and downhill at safe speeds.

For advanced skating technique tips, see some of the Comments sections in the advanced workouts in chapters 8 through 11.

Practice is critical for the development of proper technique. It not only gets you accustomed to doing the movements in the correct

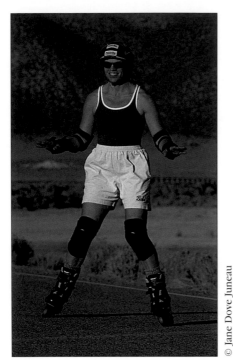

© Jane Dove Juneau

© Jane Dove Juneau

An A-frame turn provides the beginner with stability.

A parallel turn improves maneuverability and resembles your body's natural stance.

way, but also helps build the muscle strength to allow you to move on to developing a more efficient stride. It isn't uncommon to take two to three months of training before the muscles are developed to a degree that will allow optimum skating technique. Practicing a skill without sufficient strength to perform it properly is counterproductive; you'll not only learn to do the skill incorrectly but also may injure yourself. Make sure you spend enough time training at an intensity level that is not too strenuous for you in order to develop the strength necessary to properly execute the skills outlined above.

5

Warming Up and Cooling Down

Warming up, stretching, and cooling down enhance performance in many ways. In this chapter you'll learn the difference between warming up and stretching and how to cool down properly, elements that will set you up for workout success!

Warming Up

Before starting to exercise, it's wise practice to perform a low-level activity that results in a "warming up" of the body. Normally, a warm-up is done actively rather than passively. An example of a passive warm-up is sitting in a dry sauna room until perspiration starts to build on your forehead. There is no proof that this type of "warming up" is beneficial, or even that it limits the risk of injury. Active warm-up, on the other hand, can include anything from walking briskly to skating slowly to jogging, and should result in a slight increase in breathing and heart rate as well as in the temperature of the muscles you will be using for your activity. Perspiration is usually a sign of adequate warm-up as well, although in warmer, more humid climates or colder conditions that may not be the case.

In some respects, exercising without warming up first is like driving your car with the brakes on; you'll encounter unnecessary resistance to movement. A simple explanation of why this occurs is that a muscle that has been warmed has less resistance to contraction and relaxation than an unwarmed muscle. In addition, during the first few minutes of hard-effort skating, if not warmed up properly, muscles may feel rigid, partly because blood flow is restricted.

© Jane Dove Juneau

Ease into workouts with an easy pace. Use this time to enjoy the great outdoors.

Spending as little as 5 minutes before your in-line skating workout to warm up and 5 to 10 minutes after your workout to cool down can help protect you from injury. As you get older, this becomes even more important for both performance and injury prevention, and the warm-up period should be extended. Warming up is insurance for safety; it prepares your body for the work ahead.

Research clearly shows that a reduction in athletic performance is associated with lower muscle temperatures. Physiologically, all of your bodily functions for sports performance are temperature dependent. Within the first 5 minutes of moderate-intensity activity, muscle temperatures can rise as much as four degrees Fahrenheit; in 10 minutes that figure can climb another two degrees. These warmer muscle temperatures appear to provide an environment in which the body can work more efficiently. And all of this is accomplished while the body temperature remains fairly normal. The temperature rise brought about by warm-up stimulates joint lubrication to reduce friction between the contacting surfaces, makes it easier for oxygen to be utilized by the exercising muscles, and increases both the rate and efficiency of muscular contraction and relaxation.

Another benefit of warming up, as noted, is that the moderate-intensity exercise is sufficient to initiate an increase in heart rate. This is especially important if you are going to be participating in an activity, such as in-line skating, that requires a significant increase in heart rate. Beginning to exercise without warming up—and without allowing adequate time for a gradual increase in heart rate—can be dangerous, especially for people with heart disease or other cardiovascular problems.

A gradual warm-up also helps to prevent early muscle fatigue. If your muscles are properly warmed up, the blood flow to those muscles is probably adequate to let you begin to exercise. Without adequate blood flow, fatigue and lactic acid buildup can occur earlier and at a lower workload than necessary.

Benefits of Warming Up

1. Raises internal and cellular temperatures
2. Activates energy sources within the muscles for effort
3. Stimulates a higher rate of oxygen exchange between the blood and muscles
4. Increases speed and force of muscular contraction
5. Increases muscle elasticity and range of motion

6. Can reduce the incidence of exercise-induced cardiac problems brought on by sudden increases in heart rate, blood pressure, and respiratory rate
7. Builds confidence by engendering a mental state of readiness

Three Phases of the Warm-Up

Your warm-up period should last at least five minutes, or until slight
perspiration builds up on your forehead. It can be organized into
three phases, as follows, with phase 1 or 2 *mandatory*.

1. **Nonrelated movement exercises.** These small, isolated movements include side-to-side neck rotations, shoulder shrugs, hip
isolations, ankle circles, and breathing exercises.
2. **Sport-specific movements involving coordination.** Concentrate on muscles and movements surrounding the ankles,
knees, hips, low back, and shoulders, including side reaches,
arm circles, trunk twists, half-squats, leg swings, and abduction
and adduction at the hip.

© Jane Dove Juneau

Single-leg balance is an essential skill that can be
rehearsed during the warm-up.

3. **Skill rehearsal.** Skate at an easy to moderate pace. Include drills for balance and exercises to improve your stride. This phase enhances body awareness and improves accuracy, timing, and coordination.

Stretching

Warming up and stretching do not serve the same purpose. Warming up involves muscular contraction; stretching involves the opposite—relaxing and lengthening the muscles. If you stretch before warming up, you may do more damage to your muscles than if you skated with no warm-up at all.

Stretching results in flexibility. It elongates muscles to greater than normal resting length, which increases their elastic capacity. Flexibility allows you to move freely in various directions and is the key to avoiding injury, since it permits greater range of motion within the joints, ligaments, and other connective tissues.

Why is range of motion important for in-line skating? If you watch the movements of a professional speed skater, you'll notice the low, flexed body position. Flexibility allows the skater to achieve this lower body position for a more powerful push of the working leg and a more stable balance point for longer glide on

© Jane Dove Juneau

Warm up the action leg by doing a series of push-offs with the same leg and then switch to the other leg.

the support leg. The result is efficiency and speed. This is also important for recreational skaters; you don't want to expend energy wastefully by trying to move beyond the limits of your normal range of motion.

Though ligaments and tendons have little elasticity, muscles are elastic and tend to return to their original length. Stretching over a period of time will increase your muscles' resting length. Without stretching, muscles can become short, tight, and unresponsive. When tension suddenly and forcefully contracts tight muscles, microscopic tears can occur, causing soreness or injury. This is why it's so important to warm up before stretching. Stretch with proper technique—after you've warmed up—and your body will reap the benefits with a greater range of motion for a more powerful stride.

Methods of Stretching

Possible methods of acquiring flexibility include martial arts, yoga, AIS (active isolated stretching), and PNF (proprioceptive neuromuscular facilitation). Active isolated stretching is a system designed to increase flexibility of specific joints. The stretch-reflex mechanism of muscles is employed to allow increased range of motion while protecting against injury. Joints are taken through their normal range of motion by use of the primary movement-initiating muscle, then assisted through an increased range of motion while the opposing muscle group is consciously relaxed.

Proprioceptive neuromuscular facilitation is based on the physiological supposition that opposing muscle groups relax. This technique typically employs a partner, and range of motion is increased by moving the involved limb against resistance, or after the involved muscles are fatigued. Both AIS and PNF use static (no bouncing) techniques and are beneficial in increasing range of motion. Because static stretching is practical and within the capabilities of most people, we recommend static stretches for purposes outlined in this book.

Phases of Stretching

When you stretch you should be relaxed rather than struggling to maintain balance. Although standing stretches can be effective, generally they make relaxation difficult, since some muscle tension and coordination is required to keep your body upright. Relaxation is essential in order to optimally elongate muscle fibers. Each of these stretching phases are necessary to avoid injury.

1. During the first phase, get into your initial stretch position. For example, if you're stretching your hamstrings, you'll lie on your back and extend one leg up, clasping behind your leg with both hands. This is considered a stretch position. Next, you'll establish a breathing pattern. This is the point at which the stretch begins to take place.

2. During the second phase, inhale, then exhale while applying resistance to the muscles (by pulling your leg closer to your head during the hamstring example) or pushing your leg against resistance (PNF). Thousands of nerve endings respond to this resistance by lengthening the muscle fibers. You'll feel a tingling sensation; your muscles are close to their elastic limit. Hold this position for at least 15 seconds.

3. During the final phase, take another breath and as you exhale, reapply resistance and hold again. Any pulling, straining, or shaking sensation you feel is being triggered by your ligaments and tendons, which are not elastic by nature. These sensations mean you've gone too far. Back off an inch or so.

Hamstrings stretch

Lower back/abductors stretch

Adductors stretch

Hip flexors stretch

Quads stretch

Follow these five stretches or add them to your existing stretching routine. Once proficient at in-line skating, these stretches can be performed with skates on. (Photos © Jane Dove Juneau.)

Stretch Right

Here are some quick and easy tips to remember when you initiate a stretching program. Refer to these points when you want to get a quick refresher course on how to stretch effectively.

1. Never stretch a cold muscle! Warm up first for at least 5 to 10 minutes. (The older you are, the more you'll benefit from a longer warm-up.)
2. Hold each stretch statically for at least 15 seconds.
3. Don't lock your joints; keep them slightly flexed. Locking joints can stretch ligaments and increase your risk of injury.
4. Don't bounce. Ballistic movements trick the muscles into a protective reflexive contraction that can cause microscopic tearing of the fibers.
5. Maintaining your position, slowly exhale while you stretch, and hold the position for several seconds; breathing relieves tension and allows you to slowly increase range of motion.
6. To modify stretches, change the relationship of the body with gravity (lie down, sit, or hold on to a stationary object for balance if necessary).
7. Stretch after your workout to help you cool down.

The warm-up and stretch will increase your range of motion and expand your limits for safe effort. This flexibility gives you the elastic mobility to maintain balance on skates to facilitate powerful endurance and speed.

Cooling Down

Cool-down is just as important as warm-up in many respects. Without proper cool-down, you may wind up with problems ranging from sore muscles (not enough time was spent getting all of the waste products from exercise out of the muscles in cool-down) to heart problems (due to pooling of the blood in the extremities during exercise without adequate time to let the blood recirculate).

At the end of your workout, spend 5 to 10 minutes cooling down. Bring your skating pace down to warm-up level—easy to moderate. Then, check your heart rate. When it has returned to within about 10 to 20 beats of normal, skate easy for a few minutes more or try some gentle downhill turning, then perform the same stretches as in your warm-up. If your heart rate tapers quickly back to normal, your recovery is good, and it may be time to take your training to the next zone.

PART II

IN-LINE SKATING WORKOUT ZONES

This book offers an intensity level for everyone, from moderately active individuals to competitive athletes. The chapters that follow in part II include six color-coded workout zones that are graduated in duration, intensity, and distance beginning with green, and moving on to blue, purple, yellow, orange, and red.

As the chapter numbers increase, so does the fitness level necessary to comfortably and safely complete the workouts in those chapters. The fitness level necessary for each group of chapters breaks down like this: chapters 6 and 7 (green and blue)—beginner; chapters 8 and 9 (purple and yellow)—intermediate; chapters 10 and 11 (orange and red)—advanced. This format is consistent, regardless of the duration of the workouts in the chapter. For example, chapter

8 workouts (purple zone) require a higher fitness level and more skating experience than chapter 6 workouts (green zone), even though the duration is almost the same; this is because the intensity is increased. Although chapter 7 workouts last longer (40 to 50 minutes), they require less fitness and experience than chapter 8 workouts (which last only 30 minutes), due to intensity differences.

The total number of calories burned during each workout is affected by the time skated, the distance skated, and/or the tempo (whether the skating pace was consistent or ranged from slow to fast). You'll find much variety among the workouts—everything from slow, easy skating, to sprints with a partner, to time trialing against yourself for a personal best.

The workouts in most sections are designed to progress from easier to harder; for example, workout #1 is easier than workout #2, and so on. However, this progression will not necessarily hold for everyone, especially in chapters 10 and 11, since some skaters will find it more difficult to sprint or climb hills. Also, if your local terrain forces you to substitute sprints for hill climbing, you may encounter more of a physical challenge than people who have hills available. Regardless of how you approach your training program (longer workouts one week, shorter workouts the next, or vice versa), you should be able to assemble a fun, diverse array of workouts. Don't just go through each chapter in order each time you follow the workouts; mix and match them.

A good training program doesn't focus constantly on hard, high-intensity workouts; instead, it provides for rest days and easy days. On rest days, you may not exercise at all, or switch to another activity (see the discussion on cross-training in chapter 14). On easy days, you can choose a workout from the green or blue zone. Whatever system you select, remember that one of the highest risks associated with any activity is doing too much, too soon.

Intensity Zones

The table below delineates the workout color zones and some of the variables associated with them. Note that the acronyms RPE (rating of perceived exertion) and MHR (maximum heart rate) are used here; an explanation of each is included later in this chapter.

WORKOUT COLOR ZONES

Zone (chapter)	Type of workout	RPE/ %MHR	Time
Green (6)	Low intensity, short duration	1–4/60–75	≤30 min
Blue (7)	Low intensity, long duration	1–4/60–75	40–50 min
Purple (8)	Moderate intensity, short duration	2–6/65–85	30 min
Yellow (9)	Moderate intensity, long duration	2–6/65 85	40–90 min
Orange (10)	High intensity, short duration	3–10/70–95+	≤35 min
Red (11)	High intensity, long duration	3–8+/70–95+	40–150 min

Determining Average Speed

To determine how fast you're skating, you need two items of information: the distance traveled and the time spent. Finding the total time spent skating is easy: all it requires is a timer. The best type to use is a wristwatch with a sweep second hand, or a stopwatch. It's much easier to use a stopwatch than a wristwatch, since stopwatches are designed to monitor time intervals. Start your timer when you start your warm-up (or your workout, depending on the instructions for the workout you're doing), and stop your timer when you're finished (with the workout or the cool-down, again depending on the instructions).

Determining the total distance you skate is a bit more difficult, but you have a few choices:

1. Drive in your automobile the route that you'll be skating. Note the odometer reading and measure the length of your course. This will give you a fairly accurate (within a tenth of a mile) estimate of the distance of your route.
2. Ride a bicycle outfitted with a bicycle computer (speedometer/ odometer) along your route. This is usually slightly more precise than the preceding method, assuming the computer is calibrated properly.
3. Know the route and the distance. For example, if you're skating on a path that's commonly used for bicycling and/or jogging, some indication of the total distance of the route may be posted near the starting point of the path.
4. Buy a skate speedometer/odometer and skate the route.

To calculate the average speed at which you've skated, use the following formula, inserting your total minutes skated and total miles traveled.

Skating speed formula:

60 ÷ total minutes skating × total miles traveled =
skating speed (miles per hour)

For example, during a timed workout, Suzanne skates 4.0 miles in 20 minutes. In this example, total miles traveled = 4.0, and total minutes skating = 20. Simply enter these numbers in the skating speed formula to complete the calculation.

60 ÷ 20 (minutes) × 4.0 (miles skated) =
12.0 miles per hour.

Suzanne's average speed during this training session was 12.0 miles per hour.

Or, let's say that Suzanne skates for three hours. She completes three laps of her 10-mile route. In this example, total miles traveled = 30 (three laps of 10 miles per lap), and total minutes skating = 180 (three hours × 60 minutes per hour). Substitute these numbers in the skating speed formula.

60 ÷ 180 (minutes) × 30 (miles skated) =
10 miles per hour

Suzanne's average speed during this training session was 10 miles per hour. To eliminate the necessity of performing the calculations, you can purchase a skate speedometer. These small, battery-operated computers attach easily to your skates and can display several functions, such as maximum and average speeds, total time skated, distance skated, and time.

Measuring Workout Intensity

The RPE scale or Borg Scale, as shown in table II.1, enables you to describe your own sensation of effort. Using the RPE, you can evaluate your internal "comfort zone" during your workout, basing intensity on how you feel. There are no equipment requirements, and you can check exercise intensity without stopping (unlike with traditional heart rate checks). By becoming familiar with the RPE scale, you can help ensure a level of exertion that is safe and appropriate to both your level of in-line skating fitness and your goals for conditioning.

A common question many people ask is, "What RPE intensity is appropriate for me if I want to achieve optimal benefits from my skating?" There is no single answer to that question, since it depends mainly on your goals, current fitness level, and training program's design. For example, you don't want to do two consecutive days of high-intensity training; your body should have a day or more between intense workouts to allow for recovery. Likewise, if you're training for competition, you don't want to do all low-intensity workouts; that would not prepare your body for the high-output demands of racing.

Table II.1 Borg Scale	
0	Nothing at all
0.5	Extremely weak (just noticeable)
1	Very weak
2	Weak (light)
3	Moderate
4	
5	Strong (heavy)
6	
7	Very strong
8	
9	
10	Extremely strong (almost maximal)
●	Maximal

Heart rate is another reliable method of determining the intensity of an exercise. As exercise intensity increases, your heart rate increases in response to the muscles' increased demand for oxygen as they do more work.

An easy method to monitor heart rate is palpation at the radial artery on the arm. Though it sounds complicated, palpation is simply feeling the pulsations of blood as they're being pumped with each heartbeat. Pulse is taken by placing your index and second finger on the small groove on the thumb side of the inner part of your wrist. The slight tapping you feel is your pulse. Simply count the number of taps in a 15-second period, and multiply that number by four. That is your heart rate, or pulse rate, in beats per minute. Take your resting heart rate first thing in the morning as soon as you wake up, but before getting out of bed.

An easier and more reliable method of determining heart rate is to use a heart rate monitor. Chapter 2 provides some tips on heart rate monitor selection and desirable features.

What Is an Appropriate Heart Rate?

While a number of methods are in use for determining what a person's heart rate should be during exercise, for most fitness programs, 60 to 90 percent of your maximum heart rate (MHR) or your estimated maximum heart rate (EMHR) is considered your target heart rate zone (THR). You can perform a graded exercise test administered by your physician to determine your maximum heart rate, or you can estimate the rate. Most healthy individuals with no risk factors for heart disease prefer to estimate their maximum heart rate.

Use the following formula to determine your estimated maximum heart rate (EMHR):

220 – your age (in years) = EMHR

Then use the following formula to determine your target heart rate zone (THR):

MHR or EMHR × .6 = low end of THR
MHR or EMHR × .9 = high end of THR

You can use this information when you select a training program. For example, if you're just beginning aerobic conditioning, you should aim for the low end of the target heart rate zone and pick up intensity as you establish cardiovascular fitness. If you are in good shape and want to train for competition, you'll aim for the high end of your target heart rate zone. Keep in mind that the target heart rates are suggested for healthy individuals. If you are taking medication or have an existing injury, check with your physician before proceeding.

These methods of assessing exercise intensity are only suggestions. Get in touch with your body. Exercise responsibly. If you feel as if you're working too hard, you probably are.

Estimating Caloric Expenditure

The caloric expenditure of each workout in part II has already been estimated for you; it includes the warm-up and cool-down skating time as well as the actual workout skating time. All of the calorie expenditure figures shown are based on a 150-pound skater using standard recreational skates on a flat, smooth skating surface unless the workout specifically calls for terrain such as hills. If you weigh more or less, are using racing (longer frame, four- or five-wheel) skates, or if you skate on hills when not mentioned in the workout, your calorie expenditure can vary significantly.

6

Green Zone

The purpose of the green zone is to help you comfortably achieve cardiovascular conditioning without risking overuse injury. This zone is also used for "easy day" workouts because everybody needs to rest to reap the most benefits from conditioning.

As a rule, green zone workouts raise your heart rate to 60 to 75 percent of maximum and last less than 30 minutes. It's certainly acceptable, however, to use the workouts for less than 30 minutes; 10 minutes is a great start, as long as you are consistent. Nevertheless, we do encourage you to go for at least 25 minutes to gain the most benefits. If you desire to skate and train at the competitive level, green zone workouts might even be appropriate as a warm-up before heavy training.

You'll find longer-duration versions of these workouts in the blue zone.

WORKOUT 1

1

TIMED EASY SKATE
TOTAL TIME: 25 minutes

WARM-UP: Skate easy for 5 minutes, then begin your workout.

WORKOUT

Distance/time: 15 minutes
Terrain: Flat
Pace: Easy
Speed: 9 to 10 miles per hour
Effort: RPE 1-3; 60% to 70% MHR

COOL-DOWN: Skate slowly for 3 minutes, taking some deep breaths, then stretch.
CALORIES BURNED: Approx. 210

COMMENTS

Concentrate on keeping your strokes even; the time for each complete stroke on your left leg should match the time on your right leg.

WORKOUT 2

DISTANCE EASY SKATE
TOTAL TIME: 25 minutes

WARM-UP: Skate easy for 5 minutes, then begin your workout.

WORKOUT

Distance/time: 2 to 2.5 miles
Terrain: Flat
Pace: Easy
Speed: 9 to 10 miles per hour
Effort: RPE 1-3; 60% to 70% MHR

COOL-DOWN: Skate slowly for 3 minutes, then stretch.
CALORIES BURNED: Approx. 210

COMMENTS

Using either your car or bicycle odometer, map out the distance first, then skate it. Work on your stride technique by gliding longer on the support foot. Feel for even pressure on the entire length of the bottom of the foot while gliding.

WORKOUT 3

3

TIMED INTERVALS
TOTAL TIME: 25 to 30 minutes

WARM-UP: Skate easy for 5 minutes, then begin your workout.

WORKOUT

Distance/time: 15 to 20 minutes

Terrain: Flat

Pace: Alternate timed intervals—30 seconds of slightly more intense skating interspersed with 90 seconds of easy skating.

Speed: 9 to 11 miles per hour

Effort: RPE 1-4; 60% to 75% MHR

COOL-DOWN: Skate slowly for 5 minutes, then stretch.

CALORIES BURNED: Approx. 285

COMMENTS

Doing brief intervals that are more intense gradually prepares you for greater intensity later on. Work on breathing evenly and balancing as described in chapter 4 ("Striding").

WORKOUT 4

GRADUATED INTENSITY
TOTAL TIME: 30 minutes

4

WARM-UP: Skate easy for 5 minutes, then begin your workout.

WORKOUT

Distance/time: 20 minutes

Terrain: Flat

Pace: Gradually pump harder to travel faster. You have 10 minutes to get your pace up to an intensity and speed that has you breathing harder than during your warm-up. Stay at that steady state of intensity for 10 full minutes, then begin to slow your pace down.

Speed: 9 to 11 miles per hour

Effort: RPE 2-4; 65% to 75% MHR

COOL-DOWN: Skate slowly for 5 minutes, then stretch.

CALORIES BURNED: Approx. 255

COMMENTS

Work on stride technique by concentrating on pushing off harder (to travel faster) with the legs. Maintaining a lower body position helps you do this by providing a longer skating stroke.

WORKOUT 5

5

STEADY SKATE
TOTAL TIME: 30 minutes

WARM-UP: Skate at an easy pace for 5 minutes, then begin your workout.

WORKOUT

Distance/time: 20 minutes

Terrain: Flat

Pace: Take 5 minutes to reach a somewhat strong-intensity pace, and keep going for 15 minutes at that intensity.

Speed: 9 to 11 miles per hour

Effort: RPE 1-4; 60% to 75% MHR

COOL-DOWN: Skate easy for 5 minutes, then stretch.

CALORIES BURNED: Approx. 290

COMMENTS

Think of this workout as your reward for working hard on workout #3; you get to maintain a fairly good pace without pushing yourself too much.

WORKOUT 6

TIMED INTERVALS
TOTAL TIME: 25 to 30 minutes

6

WARM-UP: Skate at an easy pace for 5 minutes, then begin your workout.

WORKOUT

Distance/time: 15 to 20 minutes

Terrain: Flat

Pace: Alternate timed intervals—1 minute of faster skating interspersed with 3 minutes of easy skating.

Speed: 9 to 11 miles per hour

Effort: RPE 1-4; 60% to 75% MHR

COOL-DOWN: Skate easy for 5 minutes, then stretch.

CALORIES BURNED: Approx. 285

COMMENTS

Don't skate too fast on your work intervals; you should be able to maintain an even pace for the full 1 minute. If you get too tired to maintain your pace during those 1-minute intervals, you're skating too fast.

WORKOUT 7

STEADY SKATE
TOTAL TIME: 30 minutes

WARM-UP: Skate at an easy pace for 5 minutes, then begin your workout.

WORKOUT

Distance/time: 20+ minutes

Terrain: Flat

Pace: Build your speed up to a moderately hard pace (RPE = 4) and maintain it for 20 minutes.

Speed: 9 to 11 miles per hour

Effort: RPE 1-4; 60% to 75% MHR

COOL-DOWN: Skate easy for 5 minutes, then stretch.

CALORIES BURNED: Approx. 275

COMMENTS

Try to relax and get comfortable; this is a longer-duration workout. It will help to prepare you for the workouts at the next level.

WORKOUT 8

TIMED INTERVALS
TOTAL TIME: 25 to 30 minutes

8

WARM-UP: Skate at an easy pace for 3 minutes, then increase the intensity to a moderate pace for an additional 3 minutes.

WORKOUT

Distance/time: 13 to 18 minutes

Terrain: Flat

Pace: Alternate timed intervals—1 minute of faster skating interspersed with 2 minutes of easy skating.

Speed: 9 to 11 miles per hour

Effort: RPE 1-4; 60% to 75% MHR

COOL-DOWN: Skate at a slightly less-than-moderate pace for 3 minutes, then at an easy pace for 3 minutes, then stretch.

CALORIES BURNED: Approx. 260

COMMENTS

Don't skate too fast on your work intervals; you should be able to maintain an even pace for the full 1 minute. If you get too tired to maintain your pace during those 1-minute intervals, you're skating too fast.

Summary Table Green Zone Workouts			
Workout	**Description**	**Duration**	**Intensity (RPE/%MHR)**
1	Timed Easy	25 minutes	1-3/60%-70%
2	Distance Easy	25 minutes	1-3/60%-70%
3	Timed Intervals	25-30 minutes	1-4/60%-75%
4	Graduated Intensity	30 minutes	2-4/65%-75%
5	Steady	30 minutes	1-4/60%-75%
6	Timed Intervals	25-30 minutes	1-4/60%-75%
7	Steady	30 minutes	1-4/60%-75%
8	Timed Intervals	25-30 minutes	1-4/60%-75%

7

Blue Zone

Blue zone workouts are similar to green zone workouts but are of longer duration. Since you're developing some endurance, you'll be skating longer—from 40 to 50 minutes per workout session. These workouts provide you with more cardiovascular endurance. We'll also focus a bit more on your technique, especially balance, use of your arms, and longer strides and backward skating for maneuverability.

By this time, your skating skills are getting more efficient. You are more comfortable going faster, and you may be considering spending more time in your workouts. You may also want to use the additional endurance to help with your cross-training activities (see chapter 14). You can duplicate the duration of these workouts with your cross-training activities.

WORKOUT 1

1

TIMED EASY SKATE
TOTAL TIME: 40 minutes

WARM-UP: Skate easy for 5 minutes, then begin your workout.

WORKOUT

Distance/time: 30 minutes
Terrain: Flat
Pace: Easy
Speed: 9 to 10 miles per hour
Effort: RPE 1-3; 60% to 70% MHR

COOL-DOWN: Skate slowly for 5 minutes, then stretch.
CALORIES BURNED: Approx. 380

COMMENTS

During your warm-up, experiment with balance on your support foot. Start by feeling your body weight on the ball of the foot to the middle of your foot, and very gradually shift your hips so that you feel that most of your body weight is on your heels. Return to the middle of your foot to reestablish comfortable balance.

WORKOUT 2

DISTANCE EASY SKATE
TOTAL TIME: 40 to 45 minutes

2

WARM-UP: Skate easy on flat terrain for 5 minutes.

WORKOUT

Distance/time: Approx. 5 to 6 miles
Terrain: Flat
Pace: Skate at a comfortable pace.
Speed: 9 to 10 miles per hour
Effort: RPE 1-3; 60% to 70% MHR

COOL-DOWN: Skate slowly for 5 minutes, then stretch.
CALORIES BURNED: Approx. 430

COMMENTS

For both the first 5 minutes and last 5 minutes, practice balancing on each foot a little longer during the glide phase of your stride. As the other foot returns from its push-off, keep it just above the ground for safety. For better balance, keep your hands in front so you can see them with your peripheral vision.

WORKOUT 3

3

TIMED INTERVALS
TOTAL TIME: 40 to 45 minutes

WARM-UP: Skate easy on flat terrain for 5 minutes.

WORKOUT

Distance/time: 30 to 35 minutes

Terrain: Flat

Pace: Alternate timed, increased-pace intervals of 30 seconds each with continuous easy skating. Intervals should be done every 3 to 4 minutes.

Speed: 9 to 11 miles per hour

Effort: RPE 1-4; 60% to 75% MHR

COOL-DOWN: Skate slowly for 5 minutes, then stretch. During your cool-down, reach up toward the sky and inhale. Take a few exhilarating deep breaths. As you reach, release energy from your fingertips. Pull both arms in front of you to stretch your back muscles.

CALORIES BURNED: Approx. 400

COMMENTS

To skate faster during the intervals, pump your arms in opposition to your feet (left foot forward, right arm forward). Swing arms forward and backward, not side to side. Relax your hands as you swing your arms.

WORKOUT 4

GRADUATED INTENSITY
TOTAL TIME: 40 to 45 minutes

4

WARM-UP: Skate easy on flat terrain for 5 minutes.

WORKOUT

Distance/time: 30 to 35 minutes

Terrain: Flat

Pace: Move from an easy skate gradually to more intensity. Take 10 minutes to reach a moderate pace and intensity, then skate at that pace for 15 to 20 minutes. Take 5 minutes to gradually bring the pace back down to a comfortable intensity.

Speed: 9 to 11 miles per hour

Effort: RPE 1-4; 60% to 75% MHR

COOL-DOWN: Skate slowly for 5 minutes, then stretch.

CALORIES BURNED: Approx. 440

COMMENTS

During your warm-up, experiment with the pressure you feel along the sole of the foot of your action/push-off leg. Push off first at the ball of your foot, then the middle of the foot, then the heel. Continue to be aware of where the pressure along the foot lies, and keep the pressure on the whole inside edge of the foot.

WORKOUT 5

TIMED STEADY SKATE
TOTAL TIME: 50 minutes

WARM-UP: Skate easy on flat terrain for 5 minutes.

WORKOUT

Distance/time: 40 minutes

Terrain: Flat

Pace: Take 5 minutes to get to a pace that has you breathing somewhat harder than during the warm-up. Stay at that steady pace on flat terrain for approximately 35 minutes.

Speed: 9 to 10 miles per hour

Effort: RPE 1-3; 60% to 75% MHR

COOL-DOWN: Skate slowly for 5 minutes, then stretch.

CALORIES BURNED: Approx. 475

COMMENTS

During your warm-up, practice skating more upright, then more crouched. Feel the changes in tension in the muscles in your legs and the pressure changes at your knees and ankles. As you push off, extend the push-off leg completely, bringing your foot back in a circular motion behind you and gently placing it directly under your hips. Notice how much more powerful you feel when your body is more compact. Remember to pace yourself; this is not a high-intensity workout.

WORKOUT 6

TIMED INTERVALS
TOTAL TIME: 45 minutes

6

WARM-UP: Skate easy on flat terrain for 10 minutes.

WORKOUT

Distance/time: 30 minutes

Terrain: Flat

Pace: Take 5 minutes to reach a somewhat intense pace, then add seven intervals of 1 minute each, with 3 minutes of slower skating between each interval, for a total time of 30 minutes.

Speed: 9 to 11 miles per hour

Effort: RPE 1-4; 60% to 75% MHR

COOL-DOWN: Skate slowly for 5 minutes, then stretch.

CALORIES BURNED: Approx. 495

COMMENTS

During your warm-up, practice going from skating forward to skating backward to skating forward again, for maneuverability. This will add some fun to the workout.

WORKOUT 7

DISTANCE SKATE
TOTAL TIME: 45 to 50 minutes

WARM-UP: Skate easy on flat terrain for 5 minutes.

WORKOUT

Distance/time: 6.2 miles
Terrain: Flat or rolling
Pace: Skate at a moderate pace.
Speed: 10 to 11 miles per hour
Effort: RPE 2-4; 65% to 75% MHR

COOL-DOWN: Skate slowly for 5 minutes, then stretch.
CALORIES BURNED: Approx. 480

COMMENTS

Concentrate on maintaining good skating form; take nice, long strides. Don't let your form deteriorate. If you're tired, try a few shorter strides and then return to longer strides, to use slightly different muscles. After completing this workout, you should be confident enough to get involved with a 10K fun roll; you've just completed your first 10K distance!

WORKOUT 8

TIMED SKATE
TOTAL TIME: 50 minutes

WARM-UP: Skate easy on flat terrain for 5 minutes.

WORKOUT

Distance/time: 40 minutes
Terrain: Flat
Pace: Skate at an easy to moderate pace.
Speed: 9 to 10 miles per hour
Effort: RPE 2-3; 65% to 70% MHR

COOL-DOWN: Skate slowly for 5 minutes, then stretch.
CALORIES BURNED: Approx. 380

COMMENTS

Make sure you keep this skate at a comfortable, easy to moderate pace. This is a workout to which you can return even when you're doing orange and red zone workouts, as a break from a more intense workout schedule.

Summary Table Blue Zone Workouts			
Workout	**Description**	**Duration**	**Intensity (RPE/%MHR)**
1	Timed Easy	40 minutes	1-3/60%-70%
2	Distance Easy	40-45 minutes	1-3/60%-70%
3	Timed Intervals	40-45 minutes	1-4/60%-75%
4	Graduated Intensity	40-45 minutes	1-4/60%-75%
5	Timed Steady	50 minutes	1-3/60%-75%
6	Timed Intervals	45 minutes	1-4/60%-75%
7	Distance	45-50 minutes	2-4/65%-75%
8	Timed	50 minutes	2-3/65%-70%

8

Purple Zone

Purple zone workouts can be considered intermediate-level workouts. While green zone workouts focus on getting you onto your skates for some time and distance at an easy pace, and blue zone workouts add some technique, purple zone workouts focus on both increasing intensity and paying attention to your skating technique. We will also introduce you to skating with a partner.

The many benefits of skating with a partner include having someone with you who can help make you work harder, providing a critical eye to help improve your skating technique, and last but not least, making skating workouts more fun. Try to get someone whose fitness and skill level is similar to yours, since it can be difficult skating with someone of a much higher or lower fitness level. Skating with someone of a different fitness or skating ability is possible if the slower or less fit skater drafts behind the faster or more fit skater. In this way, you decrease the amount of work being done by the person drafting, making it easier to maintain a given pace.

WORKOUT 1

1

TIMED SKATE
TOTAL TIME: 30 minutes

WARM-UP: Skate easy on flat terrain for 5 minutes.

WORKOUT

Distance/time: 20 minutes
Terrain: Flat or rolling
Pace: Keep your skating at a moderate pace.
Speed: 9 to 12 miles per hour
Effort: RPE 2-5; 65% to 75% MHR

COOL-DOWN: Skate slowly for 3 minutes, taking some deep breaths, then stretch.
CALORIES BURNED: Approx. 335

COMMENTS

For partner workouts, skate side by side with your partner. Try to duplicate each other's stroke rate and stride technique while not looking at each other. Skating next to each other (whenever conditions permit) will force you to match stroke rates.

WORKOUT 2

DISTANCE SKATE
TOTAL TIME: 30 minutes

2

WARM-UP: Skate easy on flat terrain for 5 minutes.

WORKOUT

Distance/time: 4 miles
Terrain: Flat
Pace: Comfortable
Speed: 9 to 12 miles per hour
Effort: RPE 2-5; 65% to 75% MHR

COOL-DOWN: Skate slowly for 5 minutes, taking some deep breaths, then stretch.
CALORIES BURNED: Approx. 335

COMMENTS

Remember to pump your arms forward and backward to increase your leg speed and stroke rate. For partner workouts, see if you can "hook up" with your partner skating directly behind you by grasping his or her hand with one of your hands. Make sure you don't squeeze too hard, and try to keep in stride with your partner, matching strokes.

WORKOUT 3

3

TIMED INTERVALS
TOTAL TIME: 30 minutes

WARM-UP: Skate easy on flat terrain for 5 minutes. During the warm-up skating period, reach upward and stretch your lower back, shoulders, and arms. Reach to the side and do the same thing. Clasp hands in front to stretch your upper-back muscles, then clasp them behind. Take a few exhilarating deep breaths and prepare yourself mentally for the tough work ahead—intervals.

WORKOUT

Distance/time: 20 minutes of 30- and 90-second intervals
Terrain: Flat
Pace: Alternate timed, increased-pace intervals of 30 seconds each with continuous easy skating for 90 seconds.
Speed: 10 to 13 miles per hour
Effort: RPE 3-6; 70% to 85% MHR

COOL-DOWN: Duplicate your warm-up, then stretch.
CALORIES BURNED: Approx. 245

COMMENTS

Between intervals, consider skating upright for several seconds to give your lower back a rest. During intervals, accelerate to speed gradually—don't sprint; remember that this is an intermediate-level workout.

WORKOUT 4

GRADUATED INTENSITY
TOTAL TIME: 30 minutes

WARM-UP: Skate easy on flat terrain for 5 minutes. During the warm-up skating period, practice sitting lower as you skate by bending your knees and getting your hips as low to the ground as you can while skating efficiently. This will increase your range of motion for the workout.

WORKOUT

Distance/time: 20 to 22 minutes

Terrain: Flat

Pace: Move from an easy skate gradually to more intensity. Take 2 to 3 minutes to reach a moderately fast pace. Skate at that pace for 15 minutes, and increase your pace again smoothly at the end for the final 2 to 3 minutes.

Speed: 9 to 13 miles per hour

Effort: RPE 2-6; 65% to 85% MHR

COOL-DOWN: Bring your pace down to a comfortable level, and skate upright for at least 1 to 2 minutes while cooling down.

CALORIES BURNED: Approx. 355

COMMENTS

Now that you are gaining more in-line skating experience, it's more appropriate to move pressure along the soles of your feet a little closer to the hills. If you find your form deteriorating, skate upright for 10 to 15 seconds, and then get back into the proper position and continue skating.

WORKOUT 5

TIMED STEADY SKATE
TOTAL TIME: 30 minutes

WARM-UP: Skate easy on flat terrain for 5 minutes. During the warm-up skating period, pay particular attention to your breathing pattern: it should be relaxed and deep, not labored and shallow. Take a few deep breaths, and feel your upper body relax.

WORKOUT

Distance/time: 20 minutes

Terrain: Flat

Pace: Take 2 to 3 minutes to get to a pace that has you breathing much harder than during the warm-up. Stay at that pace for 17 to 18 more minutes.

Speed: 9 to 13 miles per hour

Effort: RPE 3-6; 70% to 85% MHR

COOL-DOWN: Bring your pace down to a comfortable level during the first 1 to 2 minutes, then skate upright for the final 3 to 4 minutes while slowing down.

CALORIES BURNED: Approx. 350

COMMENTS

Don't let anything break your concentration; maintain the pace you choose for the entire workout. As you get further into the workout, focus again on a nonlabored breathing pattern. This workout should be a somewhat hard effort but still allow natural and deep breathing. The breathing pattern used during this workout can help recovery during races, just after the pace has become faster: recall the feeling you experienced during this workout and adopt the same relaxed breathing pattern to make your breaths more efficient.

WORKOUT 6

TIMED INTERVALS
TOTAL TIME: 30 minutes

6

WARM-UP: Skate easy on flat terrain for 5 minutes. Near the end of your warm-up, pick up your pace for a minute or so, skating upright and breathing deeply while stretching the upper back, shoulders, and arms.

WORKOUT

Distance/time: 20 minutes

Terrain: Flat

Pace: Increase your pace gradually to a moderate intensity. Do eight intervals of 30 seconds each, followed by 2 minutes of slower skating between each interval.

Speed: 10 to 13 miles per hour

Effort: RPE 3-6; 70% to 85% MHR

COOL-DOWN: Skate easy for 5 minutes, stretching your arms above your head and crossing them over in front of you several times to stretch the upper-back muscles.

CALORIES BURNED: Approx. 290

COMMENTS

During the slower-skating phase of each interval, assess your posture. You should not be skating in an upright position. Tense your abdominal muscles to protect your back as you strive for a more dynamic and lower upper-body position.

WORKOUT 7

7

DISTANCE SKATE
TOTAL TIME: 30 minutes

WARM-UP: Skate easy on flat terrain for 5 minutes.

WORKOUT

Distance/time: 4 to 4.5 miles
Terrain: Flat
Pace: Skate at a moderate pace.
Speed: 9 to 13 miles per hour
Effort: RPE 2-6; 65% to 85% MHR

COOL-DOWN: Skate slowly for 5 minutes, then stretch.
CALORIES BURNED: Approx. 365

COMMENTS

Keep your thoughts focused on reaching each mile marker in a predetermined time. For example, if your goal is 4 miles, you should reach each marker in 5 minutes; if your goal is to do 4.5 miles, you need to reach each mile in approximately 4 minutes and 27 seconds.

WORKOUT 8

TIMED SKATE
TOTAL TIME: 30 minutes

8

WARM-UP: Skate easy on flat terrain for 5 minutes. During your warm up, concentrate on flexing lower and extending your leg as far to the side as you can during push-off.

WORKOUT

Distance/time: 20 minutes
Terrain: Flat
Pace: Skate at a moderate but consistent pace.
Speed: 9 to 12 miles per hour
Effort: RPE 2-5; 65% to 80% MHR

COOL-DOWN: Skate slowly for 5 minutes, then stretch.
CALORIES BURNED: Approx. 335

COMMENTS

This workout should be a welcome change from the intense intervals and distance skate earlier in this zone. Consider yourself a fairly good skater if you can complete the workouts to this point.

Summary Table Purple Zone Workouts			
Workout	**Description**	**Duration**	**Intensity (RPE/%MHR)**
1	Timed	30 minutes	2-5/65%-75%
2	Distance	30 minutes	2-5/65%-75%
3	Timed Intervals	30 minutes	3-6/70%-85%
4	Graduated Intensity	30 minutes	2-6/65%-85%
5	Timed Steady	30 minutes	3-6/70%-85%
6	Timed Intervals	30 minutes	3-6/70%-85%
7	Distance	30 minutes	2-6/65%-85%
8	Timed	30 minutes	2-5/65%-80%

9

Yellow Zone

Yellow zone workouts are classified as intermediate and also focus on partner workouts. We introduce you to sprint intervals with direction changes, including backward skating. Be sure that you practice skating backward in a safe area (a parking lot or other area free of potholes, gravel, pedestrians, and vehicles) before implementing these techniques in your training program.

In the yellow zone, workouts are extended to help develop muscular endurance as well as cardiorespiratory fitness.

WORKOUT 1

TIMED SKATE

TOTAL TIME: 60 to 70 minutes

WARM-UP: Skate easy for 5 minutes, then begin your workout.

WORKOUT

Distance/time: 50 to 55 minutes
Terrain: Flat
Pace: Take 5 minutes to work up to a moderate pace, and stay there.
Speed: 9 to 12 miles per hour
Effort: RPE 2-5; 65% to 80% MHR

COOL-DOWN: Skate slowly for 5 minutes, then stretch.
CALORIES BURNED: Approx. 670

COMMENTS

If you are partner skating, practice changing positions with your partner; while one of you "pulls" in front, the other drafts behind. Change places every 5 minutes, concentrating on making a smooth transition from being in the front to moving behind your partner. This technique is helpful during races and long skate outings; drafting can help you skate farther and/or faster than you can skate by yourself.

If you aren't partner skating, every 5 minutes check to see if your stroke rate is the same. Use the second hand on your watch or a stopwatch to count the number of strokes with each leg for a full minute. Keep track of your stroke rate, and see if it changes as you skate longer. If you notice that your stroke rate is getting noticeably faster or slower, you may be modifying your technique unconsciously, which is sometimes a sign of fatigue. If this is the case, you need to get more strength work (try doing a few more purple zone workouts).

WORKOUT 2

DISTANCE SKATE

TOTAL TIME: 55 to 65 minutes

WARM-UP: Skate easy on flat terrain for 5 minutes, then begin your workout.

WORKOUT

Distance/time: 10 miles

Terrain: Flat, or with no more than a few moderately rolling hills

Pace: Increase your skating speed within 3 to 4 minutes, then skate at a moderately hard pace.

Speed: 9 to 12 miles per hour

Effort: RPE 2-5; 65% to 80% MHR

COOL-DOWN: Skate slowly for 5 minutes, then stretch. While cooling down, stretch your arms and shoulders, breathing deeply while you stretch each muscle group.

CALORIES BURNED: Approx. 735

COMMENTS

One of the major benefits of this distance workout is that it helps you develop a constant pace, so try to be consistent. If you are partner skating and approach a hill during this workout, let your partner get 20 to 30 feet ahead of you well in advance of the hill in order for you to really see the effect that the hill has on your speed. As your partner starts to climb, you'll get much closer—because he or she is slowing down. Likewise, as your partner begins to descend the other side of the hill, the distance from you will increase as your partner speeds up.

WORKOUT 3

TIMED INTERVALS
(with backward skating)

TOTAL TIME: 40 to 60 minutes

WARM-UP: Skate easy on flat terrain for 5 minutes, then begin your workout.

WORKOUT

Distance/time: 30 to 40 minutes

Terrain: Flat to slightly rolling

Pace: Take 10 minutes to reach a moderate pace. During the next 15 minutes, do five intervals of 1 minute of faster (RPE = 6) skating to 2 minutes of slower (RPE = 4) skating. For the remaining time, alternate 1 minute of skating backward with 3-minute bouts of moderately easy skating (RPE = 3) forward.

Speed: 9 to 13 miles per hour

Effort: RPE 2-6; 65% to 85% MHR

COOL-DOWN: Skate slowly for 5 minutes, then stretch.

CALORIES BURNED: Approx. 585

COMMENTS

Your backward pace should be slower than forward skating, until you've done this workout several times. A tip on skating backward: remember that you are not interested in speed while skating backward; you are more interested in control. After you gain confidence skating backward, you will naturally pick up your speed as your technique becomes more efficient and you learn to use only the muscles necessary to skate backward.

WORKOUT 4

GRADUATED INTENSITY SKATE
TOTAL TIME: 65 to 80 minutes

WARM-UP: Skate easy on flat terrain for 5 minutes, then begin your workout.

WORKOUT

Distance/time: 55 to 70 minutes

Terrain: Flat to slightly rolling

Pace: During the first 5 minutes gradually increase pace from relatively easy to a moderate intensity. The next 5 minutes increase to a moderately hard intensity. Continue at this pace for 40 to 55 minutes, before slowing down.

Speed: 9 to 12 miles per hour

Effort: RPE 2-5; 65% to 80% MHR

COOL-DOWN: Skate slowly for 5 minutes, then stretch. If you are partner skating, have your partner comment on your technique during cool-down: Are you pushing with your toes? Are you inadvertently pushing backward as well as sideways? If you're skating alone, try to keep the same technique that you used during the workout, and check your own form for technique imperfections.

CALORIES BURNED: Approx. 835

COMMENTS

While skating, concentrate on your form, making sure you are pushing equally with both legs; don't let one leg push harder than the other as you get tired. If you're having trouble pushing with either one or both of your legs, stand up and skate in an upright position for 30 seconds, then get back into a more compact, lower position and continue. After a few sessions like this, you'll be skating consistently with both legs.

WORKOUT 5

TIMED SKATE

TOTAL TIME: 70 minutes

WARM-UP: Skate easy on flat terrain for 5 minutes.

WORKOUT

Distance/time: 60 minutes

Terrain: Flat to slightly rolling

Pace: Take 5 minutes to get to a pace that has you breathing quite a bit harder than during the warm-up. Increase your pace until you reach a moderate exertion level and keep it there. Stay at that steady pace for an additional 55 minutes.

Speed: 9 to 12 miles per hour

Effort: RPE 2-5; 65% to 80% MHR

COOL-DOWN: Skate slowly for 5 minutes, then stretch.

CALORIES BURNED: Approx. 860

COMMENTS

If you are partner skating, have your partner watch your back to see that it stays low to the ground and doesn't bob up and down. Switch who is in front pulling and who is in the rear drafting every mile or so. Concentrate on smooth transitions from the front to the rear; as you drop back to let your partner be in front, don't slow down too much, or you'll need to work harder to get back in stride behind. If you are skating alone, concentrate on watching your shadow; it will tell you a lot about your body position. Watch to see that your back is almost parallel to the ground, just as if a partner were critiquing you. Since you cannot practice changing who is in the lead if you're skating alone, practice changing your stroke rate occasionally to mimic the effort you would expend in trying to get back in stride behind someone else.

WORKOUT 6

LONG, SLOW DISTANCE SKATE

TOTAL TIME: 60 to 70 minutes

6

WARM-UP: Skate easy on flat terrain for 5 minutes, stretching your arms and upper back and making sure your neck is relaxed.

WORKOUT

Distance/time: 10 to 12 miles
Terrain: Flat to slightly rolling
Pace: Skate at a moderately hard pace.
Speed: 9 to 12 miles per hour
Effort: RPE 2-5; 65% to 80% MHR

COOL-DOWN. Skate slowly for 5 minutes, then stretch.
CALORIES BURNED: Approx. 870

COMMENTS

If you're partner skating, set your distance goal before you begin. The skater with the higher fitness level should be in the lead for any portion of the workout that feels too difficult for the less fit partner. Don't make the mistake of keeping quiet if you're working too hard; let your partner know, and switch positions. This workout is a good camaraderie builder because you need to work together to maximize your results.

If you're doing this workout alone, pay particular attention to your mile markers and your anticipated time at each marker. If you begin falling behind pace, you can pick up your speed during the next mile; if you're going too fast, you can take a little breather. Keeping track of your performance in this workout is a good way to gauge your endurance level. If you find that you're having a difficult time maintaining your pace near the end of the workout, you may want to focus more on endurance by repeating these yellow zone workouts before moving on to another workout zone.

WORKOUT 7

7

TIMED INTERVALS
(with passing drills)

TOTAL TIME: 60 minutes

WARM-UP: Skate easy on flat terrain for 5 minutes.

WORKOUT

Distance/time: 45 minutes

Terrain: Fairly flat

Pace: Spend the first 5 minutes of your workout increasing your speed to a moderately hard pace, then do 10 intervals of 1 minute of harder skating (RPE = 5) and 3 minutes of recovery (RPE = 3).

Speed: 9 to 12 miles per hour

Effort: RPE 2-5; 65% to 80% MHR

COOL-DOWN: Skate slowly for 5 minutes, then stretch.

CALORIES BURNED: Approx. 570

COMMENTS

At the beginning of each 1-minute interval, if you are partner skating you should practice passing your partner and having him or her catch up to you to finish the interval; then you can both recover during the 3-minute recovery phase. This workout provides good preparation for races in that it gives you practice at picking up your pace intermittently and catching up to someone (your partner). If you're skating alone, imagine a skater in front of you who has just picked up his or her pace; your goal is to catch that person and stay at that increased pace for a full minute, then reduce your pace slightly for 3 minutes of recovery.

WORKOUT 8

ENDURANCE SKATE
TOTAL TIME: 90 minutes

WARM-UP: Skate easy on flat terrain for 5 minutes.

WORKOUT

Distance/time: 80 minutes

Terrain: Flat

Pace: Skate at a moderately intense pace continuously. Select a pace that feels comfortable yet somewhat challenging; if you go too hard for the first 30 minutes, you'll have a difficult time finishing the entire workout. If you're partner skating, let the partner with the higher fitness level be the lead skater for most of the workout.

Speed: 9 to 12 miles per hour

Effort: RPE 2-5; 65% to 80% MHR

COOL-DOWN: Skate slowly for 5 minutes, then stretch.

CALORIES BURNED: Approx. 1,135

COMMENTS

This is the longest workout in this book. Don't underestimate the difficulty of skating for 80 minutes at an RPE of 5; it can be quite challenging. Be sure to drink plenty of fluids before beginning the workout, and carry a water bottle and something to eat to help keep you hydrated and well fueled. Good choices for energy replacement are energy bars, raisins, dates, figs, and fluid replacement beverages. See what works best for you. After you've mastered this workout, you're ready for just about any endurance challenge on in-line skates.

Workout	Description	Duration	Intensity (RPE/%MHR)
1	Timed	60-70 minutes	2-5/65%-80%
2	Distance	55-65 minutes	2-5/65%-80%
3	Timed Intervals (with backward skating)	40-60 minutes	2-6/65%-85%
4	Graduated Intensity	65-80 minutes	2-5/65%-80%
5	Timed	70 minutes	2-5/65%-80%
6	LSD	60-70 minutes	2-5/65%-80%
7	Timed Intervals (with passing)	60 minutes	2-5/65%-80%
8	Endurance	90 minutes	2-5/65%-80%

10

Orange Zone

The workouts in this chapter are much more intense than the "somewhat moderate" pace that you experienced in the purple and yellow zones. In fact, orange zone workouts are the only workouts that will make you truly reach maximal exertion levels. Because you will be working so hard during orange zone workouts and focusing your energy on skating, you won't be able to concentrate on your surroundings quite as well as you can during lower-intensity workouts. For this reason, during these workouts it is more important that you have a safe, traffic free environment in which to skate.

Orange zone workouts are limited to 35 minutes or less, since the intensity causes fatigue to set in quickly. Prior to beginning any of the orange zone workouts, you'll be doing longer warm-ups in order to avoid injury and muscle soreness.

Note: All skating speed ratings for these workouts and those in chapter 11 are based on a standard five-wheel or extended four-wheel frame. The top speeds listed are very difficult to achieve with a recreational four-wheel skate.

WORKOUT 1

1

TIMED HILL CLIMB
TOTAL TIME: 35 minutes

WARM-UP: Skate easy on flat terrain for 5 minutes. If you will be replacing the hill climbing with gradual-acceleration sprints, increase the warm-up period to 10 minutes, and spend the final 5 minutes practicing a deep-crouched skating position.

WORKOUT

Distance/time: 25 minutes

Terrain: Hilly (or one hill)

Pace: Depending on the length of the hill you will be climbing, your number of hill climbs will vary, but continuously skate uphill at an RPE of 8, then coast downhill. During the last 10 minutes, increase your pace uphill to an RPE of 9.

Speed: 10 to 14 miles per hour (your speed will depend on whether or not you're climbing a hill, and if the hill is steep)

Effort: RPE 3-9; 70% to 90% MHR

COOL-DOWN: Skate slowly for 3 minutes, taking some deep breaths, then stretch.

CALORIES BURNED: Approx. 435

COMMENTS

When climbing, practice taking shorter-than-usual strokes and using your arms to help "drive" you up the hill. Pay particular attention to your rhythm: both legs should be driving at about the same rate.

After coasting or turning to the bottom of the hill, make sure your heart rate has recovered to a pulse of no more than 20 to 30 beats above resting before you begin your next hill climb. Also, rate your breathing and fatigue on the RPE scale; they should be below 5 before you begin another climb.

WORKOUT 2

SHORT UPHILL INTERVALS
TOTAL TIME: 15 to 35 minutes

2

WARM-UP: Skate easy on flat terrain for 5 minutes. Spend another 5 minutes practicing a deep-crouched skating position.

WORKOUT

Distance/time: Depending on the length of the hill you are climbing, the total time of your workout will vary. Do six to eight hill climbs, recovering between climbs by coasting back downhill. Keep track of your times, and try to keep the total time for each climb within a few seconds of the time for your first climb.

Terrain: Hilly (or one hill)

Pace: Climb the hills at your maximum intensity. Recover downhill or by skating around the bottom of the hill until your heart rate is no more than 20 to 30 beats above resting, or your RPE = 3.

Speed: 10 to 14 miles per hour (your speed will depend on whether or not you're climbing a hill, and if the hill is steep)

Effort: RPE 3-10; 70% to 95+% MHR

COOL-DOWN: Skate slowly for 3 minutes, taking some deep breaths, then stretch.

CALORIES BURNED: Approx. 450

COMMENTS

Don't start your climbs by skating too fast at the bottom of the hill, especially on longer hills; you'll fatigue much too quickly. Climbing is a very technical aspect of skating; if you go too hard at the bottom, you'll have a tough time finishing. Pace yourself, keeping in mind the total distance of the climb.

WORKOUT 3

3

UPHILL PACE WITH TIMED INTERVALS
TOTAL TIME: 30 to 35 minutes

WARM-UP: Skate easy-moderate on flat terrain for 5 minutes. If you will be doing your skating uphill, after 3 minutes speed up a few times to a moderately hard pace. If you will be replacing uphill skating with sprints, spend another 5 minutes warming up, and make the pace of the sprints more intense (RPE = 6-7).

WORKOUT

Distance/time: 20 minutes

Terrain: Long hill

Pace: You may have difficulty finding a long enough hill for this workout; depending on the length of the hill available, you should spend 1 minute climbing hard (RPE = 9), then 2 minutes climbing easier (RPE = 4-5) Do this for a total of seven 1-minute intervals skating hard. If you are doing sprints instead of the hill climb, maintain the same intensity as if you were climbing a hill.

Speed: 11 to 14 miles per hour (your speed will depend on whether or not you're climbing a hill, and if the hill is steep)

Effort: RPE 4-9; 75% to 90+% MHR

COOL-DOWN: Skate slowly for 5 minutes, spending the last 2 minutes concentrating on a full extension of the action/pushing leg. Stretch afterwards.

CALORIES BURNED: Approx. 470

COMMENTS

Be very aware of how your legs feel during this workout. If you notice any unusual discomfort in your thighs (more than the usual fatigue that you would expect from such a workout), you should do the hill climb at a constant intensity (RPE = 5-7).

WORKOUT 4

RANDOM INTERVAL TRAINING
TOTAL TIME: 35 minutes

WARM-UP: Skate easy to moderate on flat terrain for 5 minutes. Skate for 5 additional minutes, changing your body position from crouching to upright.

WORKOUT

Distance/time: 20 minutes

Terrain: Flat or rolling

Pace: This workout is best accomplished with a partner. There is no set schedule for the intervals. When either partner feels an adequate amount of recovery from each sprint interval, he or she should try to skate away from the other person and stay away for at least 15 seconds. Each sprint interval should be rated at a 10 on the RPE scale. Make sure your recovery RPE is no higher than 3 or 4.

Speed: 10 to 20+ miles per hour

Effort: RPE 3-10; 70% to 95+% MHR

COOL-DOWN: Skate slowly for 5 minutes, stretching the upper body, arms, and lower back. Stretch afterward; a 10-minute easy skate after this workout is a good idea to assist in recovery.

CALORIES BURNED: Approx. 360

COMMENTS

As your fitness level improves, you will be able to randomly sprint away from your partner more frequently, and with less rest. You should slow down and wait for your partner if you get away for more than 30 seconds; this is an intensity workout, not an endurance workout. This workout will teach both of you to work hard to catch someone in front of you.

WORKOUT 5

10K TIME TRIAL
TOTAL TIME: 30 minutes

WARM-UP: Skate easy to moderate on flat terrain for 5 minutes. During the last 2 minutes, concentrate on your form: balance, extend your leg completely, and stay bent over so your back is almost parallel with the ground.

WORKOUT

Distance/time: 10 kilometers (6.2 miles)

Terrain: After your warm-up, go to your starting point, a spot on a trail, path, or other skate-way that is easy to find from week to week, since you will do this workout throughout the season to check your progress. The course should be a measured 10K (10 kilometers).

Pace: After spending about 1 minute getting ready, start your stopwatch, start skating, and increase your speed to your maximum sustainable pace within about 15 to 20 seconds. Maintain an RPE of 10 throughout the entire workout; this is an all-out effort!

Speed: 15 to 20+ miles per hour

Effort: RPE 10; 95+% MHR

COOL-DOWN: Skate slowly for 5 minutes, then stretch.

CALORIES BURNED: Approx. 445

COMMENTS

This is the best workout to determine your current fitness level and ability to skate hard. It's similar to the 3-mile time trial taken as your fitness evaluation test (see chapter 3), except this one is twice as far. Since this is a time trial, if you do this workout with a partner, don't draft; leave at least 10 yards between the two of you.

WORKOUT 6

GRADUATED-INTENSITY HILL CLIMB
TOTAL TIME: 35 minutes

6

WARM-UP: Skate easy to moderate on flat terrain for 5 minutes. If you will be substituting sprints for the hill climbs, skate for 5 additional minutes, changing your body position occasionally.

WORKOUT

Distance/time: 25 minutes

Terrain: Long, gradually sloping hill

Pace: Start out at a moderately intense pace (RPE = 4), increasing intensity by 1 every 2 or 3 minutes until you're skating uphill at an RPE of 10 for the last 2 minutes or so. If you're replacing the hill climbs with flat-terrain interval sprints, make each sprint 2 minutes in length, and one unit higher in intensity each time (i.e., RPE = 5 for first interval sprint, RPE = 6 for next interval sprint, etc.). Skate 1 minute at a moderate intensity (RPE = 4) between each of your sprints.

Speed: 10 to 20+ miles per hour (depending on whether you are doing hill climbing or flat terrain-interval sprints)

Effort: RPE 4-10; 75% to 95+% MHR

COOL-DOWN: Skate slowly for 5 minutes, breathing deeply while skating in a fully upright then deep-sitting position.

CALORIES BURNED: Approx. 360

COMMENTS

If you're partner skating, you can make a contest of who can go the farthest during the last 2 minutes. If you're doing sprints, make sure you spend extra time cooling down and stretching after this workout.

WORKOUT 7

TIMED INTENSE SKATE
TOTAL TIME: 35 minutes

WARM-UP: Skate easy on flat terrain for 5 minutes. During your warm-up, concentrate on making sure your weight is mostly on the rear of the foot of your action leg during each stroke. Also, concentrate on keeping your skates aimed forward during the push-off.

WORKOUT

Distance/time: 25 minutes

Terrain: Flat or slightly rolling

Pace: After a 5-minute period of increasing your skating intensity, skate for an additional 20 minutes consistently at an RPE of 8 or 9.

Speed: 10 to 18 miles per hour

Effort: RPE 3-9; 70% to 90+% MHR

COOL-DOWN: Skate slowly for 5 minutes, then stretch.

CALORIES BURNED: Approx. 495

COMMENTS

You can adjust your RPE to 8 or 9, depending on how you feel during the first few minutes of this workout.

WORKOUT 8

SHORT UPHILL INTERVALS
(with partner)
TOTAL TIME: 30 to 40 minutes

8

WARM-UP: Skate easy to moderate on flat terrain for 5 minutes. If you will be doing your skating uphill, after 3 minutes speed up a few times to a moderately hard pace. If you will be replacing uphill skating with sprints, spend another 5 minutes warming up, and do more intensely paced sprints (RPE = 6-7) during this final phase of warm-up.

WORKOUT

Distance/time: 19 minutes

Terrain: Hilly

Pace: Seven 1-minute intervals with 2 minutes recovery between. The first two intervals should be at an RPE of 8; the remaining intervals should be at an RPE of 10. The rest intervals should be performed at an RPE of 5.

Speed: 12 to 16+ miles per hour (your speed will depend on whether or not you're climbing a hill, and if the hill is steep)

Effort: RPE 5-10; 80% to 95+% MHR

COOL-DOWN: Skate slowly for 5 minutes, spending the last 2 minutes skating in a deeper-sitting position to stretch the legs. This workout may demand a second 5-minute cool-down period to allow your legs to fully recover. Stretch afterward.

CALORIES BURNED: Approx. 530

COMMENTS

This workout is one of the most intense in the book; uphill intervals require fitness and strength. This is one workout that should not be done more than once every two weeks, even during a period when you feel that you're in your peak condition.

	Summary Table Orange Zone Workouts		
Workout	**Description**	**Duration**	**Intensity (RPE/%MHR)**
1	Timed Hill Climb	35 minutes	3-9/70%-90%
2	Short Uphill Intervals	15-35 minutes	3-10/70%-95+%
3	Uphill Pace With Timed Intervals	30-35 minutes	4-9/75%-90+%
4	Random Interval Training	35 minutes	3-10/70%-95+%
5	10K Time Trial	30 minutes	10/95+%
6	Graduated-Intensity Hill Climb	35 minutes	4-10/75%-95+%
7	Timed Intense Skate	35 minutes	3-9/70%-90+%
8	Short Uphill Intervals (with partner)	30-40 minutes	5-10/80%-95+

11

Red Zone

Red zone workouts incorporate the greatest combined intensity and duration of any of the zones. This type of training is meant for people who desire to race train. Don't attempt to do these workouts before you've successfully completed the purple and yellow workouts; the intensity of red zone workouts demands that you be in good physical condition, and their duration requires significant cardiovascular endurance.

With red zone workouts, we introduce you to speed-skating techniques at race pace. You'll practice drafting, passing, and sprinting, along with some fun skating skills during the warm-up and cool-down phases.

Since you will be expending so much energy and skating for so long during these workouts, fluid replacement is especially important. Recommendations for fluid replacement are the same as those that apply to any other any intense, extended-duration workout: drink fluids prior to exercising, during exercise, and after exercise. This is of particular concern with workout #8, which can last from 2 to 2.5 hours and is the longest workout we provide.

Note: All skating speed ratings for these workouts are based on a long four-wheel or standard five-wheel frame. The top speeds listed are very difficult to achieve with a normal four-wheel skate.

WORKOUT 1

1

TIMED STEADY STATE
TOTAL TIME: 60 minutes

WARM-UP: Skate easy for 5 minutes, increase your pace to moderate (RPE = 4) for another 5 minutes, then begin your workout.

WORKOUT

Distance/time: 50 minutes

Terrain: Flat or slightly rolling

Pace: Take 5 minutes to work up to an RPE of 6, and stay there for 45 minutes.

Speed: 10 to 13 miles per hour

Effort: RPE 3-6; 70% to 85% MHR

COOL-DOWN: Skate slowly for 5 minutes, then stretch. While cooling down, stretch your arms and shoulders, breathing deeply while stretching each muscle group.

CALORIES BURNED: Approx. 815

COMMENTS

If you're partner skating, practice drafting as close behind your partner as you can. Take turns in the lead position, making your switch of position smooth. After a few position changes, notice how many strokes it takes you to get back in sync with your partner after you drop off the front.

WORKOUT 2

DISTANCE INTENSE
TOTAL TIME: 55 to 60 minutes

2

WARM-UP: Skate easy to moderate on flat terrain for 5 minutes, then begin your workout.

WORKOUT

Distance/time: 13 miles (equivalent to slightly more than two 10Ks)

Terrain: Flat to slightly hilly

Pace: Increase your skating speed within 2 to 3 minutes, then skate at a moderately hard pace (RPE = 8).

Speed: 16 to 18 miles per hour (average)

Effort: RPE 7-8; 90% to 95+% MHR

COOL-DOWN: Skate slowly for 5 minutes, then stretch. While cooling down, stretch your arms and shoulders, breathing deeply while stretching each muscle group.

CALORIES BURNED: Approx. 960

COMMENTS

To complete a workout of this intensity and duration, you will need to stay focused on your body position—specifically, staying aerodynamic. This means you'll need to keep your torso almost parallel to the ground, while maintaining your ability to breathe freely. You won't be able to complete this workout in the time allotted unless you get up to speed quickly. It helps to have a course marked every mile, so you'll know where you are relative to your goal.

WORKOUT 3

3

MODERATE SKATE WITH SPRINT TIMED INTERVALS
TOTAL TIME: 50 minutes

WARM-UP: Skate easy on flat terrain for 5 minutes. Concentrate on breathing deeply and in a relaxed way.

WORKOUT

Distance/time: 35 minutes

Terrain: Flat to moderately hilly

Pace: Take 5 minutes to reach a moderate (RPE = 4) pace. Then do seven intervals of 30 seconds of sprinting (RPE = 8) and 30 seconds of skating at an RPE of 7, with 2 minutes of slower but still moderately paced skating (RPE = 5) in between. End by alternating 1 minute skating backward with 3 minutes of moderately easy skating forward.

Speed: 11 to 16 miles per hour

Effort: RPE 4-8; 75% to 90+% MHR

COOL-DOWN: Spend the first 5 minutes of cool-down skating slowly, concentrating on stretching your arms and shoulders, then spend 5 more minutes skating easy, alternating skating in a deep-sitting position with skating upright. Stretch afterward.

CALORIES BURNED: Approx. 585

COMMENTS

During the sprints, try to accelerate slowly; don't just quickly get to top speed (rapid-acceleration sprints are done in the orange zone). Since you'll be skating for a long time in this workout, you don't want to get fatigued too soon. In a race, slowly accelerating doesn't work well unless you've just started to climb a hill; most sprints that turn into breakaways are done with rapid bursts of speed that are held for quite some time.

WORKOUT 4

GRADUATED-INTENSITY SKATE
TOTAL TIME: 60 minutes

4

WARM-UP: Skate easy on flat terrain for 5 minutes, then begin your workout.

WORKOUT

Distance/time: 50 minutes

Terrain: Flat or rolling hills

Pace: Begin at a relatively easy pace. In the first 5 minutes, move from an easy pace gradually to a moderate intensity (RPE = 4) that makes you breathe harder. Take another 5 minutes to reach a pace of moderately hard intensity (RPE = 7), and skate at that pace for 30 minutes. Take 10 minutes to gradually bring the pace back down to a comfortable intensity.

Speed: 10 to 14 miles per hour

Effort: RPE 3-7; 70% to 90% MHR

COOL-DOWN: Skate slowly for 5 minutes, then stretch.

CALORIES BURNED: Approx. 815

COMMENTS

Unless you encounter a hill or an area that makes you slow down significantly, you should always concentrate on keeping your hands in an aerodynamic position (behind your back). If you need to skate upright for a break, you can stretch your shoulders and arms briefly.

WORKOUT 5

5

DISTANCE SKATE
TOTAL TIME: 50 to 60 minutes

WARM-UP: Skate easy on flat terrain for 5 minutes.

WORKOUT

Distance/time: 12 miles

Terrain: Flat to slightly hilly

Pace: Skate at a moderately hard pace for 12 miles, spending at least 10 minutes working on passing skills (with or without a partner). Starting at the midpoint of the skate (6 miles), either pretend you're in a race and you want to pass another skater, or, if you're partner skating, actually pass your partner without looking back. You'll need to accelerate rapidly to break away from the other skater. Do this six times between the midpoint and when you finish.

Speed: 16 to 18 miles per hour

Effort: RPE 8+; 90+% MHR

COOL-DOWN: Skate slowly for 5 minutes, then stretch.

CALORIES BURNED: Approx. 960

COMMENTS

If you are not partner skating, you'll have to be very careful that you spend at least 15 to 20 seconds "passing." Make sure you move far enough to the side so that if you were actually passing someone, you'd have room for your stroke to the side. If you are partner skating, let your partner know when you'll be moving, so you don't cross skates during your passing maneuver.

WORKOUT 6

TIMED MODERATE SKATE WITH SPEEDPLAY

TOTAL TIME: 50 to 60 minutes

WARM-UP: Skate easy on flat terrain for 5 minutes, paying particular attention to your neck, shoulders, and upper back—make sure they're relaxed.

WORKOUT

Distance/time: 40 to 50 minutes

Terrain: Flat to slightly rolling

Pace: Spend the first 10 minutes gradually increasing your effort level until you reach an RPE of 8. Then, interchange skating for 2 minutes at an RPE of 8 with skating for 4 minutes at an RPE of 6. Progressively reduce the amount of time you spend skating at an RPE of 6 during each of these speedplay sessions.

Speed: 13 to 16 miles per hour

Effort: RPE 6-8; 85% to 90+% MHR

COOL-DOWN: Skate slowly for 5 to 10 minutes, then stretch.

CALORIES BURNED: Approx. 870

COMMENTS

If you're partner skating, either one of you can choose when to go to the higher RPE speed; just make sure you time yourself to do the entire 2 minutes at the higher RPE. Set your overall time goal before starting this workout. This workout should be fun, along with providing a fairly intense workout for your legs. If you're skating alone, remember to pay close attention to the amount of time you spend skating slowly; don't skate slowly for too long, or you won't get the benefits of the speed work.

WORKOUT 7

7

20K RACE PACE
TOTAL TIME: 40 to 60 minutes

WARM-UP: Skate easy on flat terrain for 5 minutes, stretching your arms and upper back. Spend the last 2 minutes of warm-up concentrating on balancing, preparing your legs for the workout.

WORKOUT

Distance/time: 20 kilometers

Terrain: Flat or slightly rolling

Pace: This workout is a simulation of a 20K skate race. You should increase your skating pace within the first 2 to 3 minutes of the workout and stay at the highest speed you can comfortably maintain.

Speed: 16 miles per hour

Effort: RPE 8; 90+% MHR

COOL-DOWN: Skate slowly for 5 minutes, then stretch.

CALORIES BURNED: Approx. 780

COMMENTS

This is not a workout you need to do more than once per month. The intensity and duration make it difficult to do on a more regular basis. If you and a partner are doing this workout together, the less fit skater can draft to maintain the pace. Don't slow down unless you absolutely need to rest; you'll find it's much easier to keep moving than to stop and then start again. If you and your partner are more evenly matched in skating fitness and ability, one of you can "go off the front" and have the other chase. It breaks up the monotony of skating for almost 1 hour at a steady pace and prepares you for what you'll encounter in races.

WORKOUT 8

50K RACE PACE
TOTAL TIME: 125 to 150 minutes
(five 10Ks at a 25-minute-per-10K pace, nonstop)

8

WARM-UP: Skate easy on flat terrain for 5 minutes. Spend more time than usual making sure you are loose and ready to skate.

WORKOUT

Distance/time: 50 kilometers (31 miles)

Terrain: Flat to slightly hilly

Pace: Begin your skate at an RPE of 7, and maintain it throughout the entire workout.

Speed: 14 miles per hour

Effort: RPE 7; 90% MHR

COOL-DOWN: Skate slowly for 5 minutes, then stretch.

CALORIES BURNED: Approx. 2,000+

COMMENTS

This workout, the granddaddy of them all, is a simulation of the long skate race—50K (31 miles). This workout shouldn't be done more than once per month due to its intensity and duration. Do this workout with a partner whenever possible. Slow down if you feel too tired; it's better to finish the workout at a slower pace than to stop completely due to excessive fatigue.

Fluid replacement is a serious concern when you're training distances of this magnitude. Make sure you're properly hydrated (drink at least one or two glasses of water 1 hour before you start the workout) and well nourished (don't eat within 1 hour of starting, but make sure you don't do the workout on an empty stomach unless you take food with you).

Summary Table Red Zone Workouts			
Workout	**Description**	**Duration**	**Intensity (RPE/%MHR)**
1	Timed Steady State	60 minutes	3-6/70%-85%
2	Distance Intense	55-60 minutes	7-8/90%-95+%
3	Moderate With Sprint Timed Intervals	50 minutes	4-8/75%-90+%
4	Graduated-Intensity	60 minutes	3-7/70%-90%
5	Distance	50-60 minutes	8+/90+%
6	Timed Moderate With Speedplay	50-60 minutes	6-8/85%-90+%
7	20K Race Pace	40-60 minutes	8/90+%
8	50K Race Pace	125-150 minutes	7/90%

PART III

TRAINING BY THE WORKOUT ZONES

Although the organization of the workout zones in part II can be interpreted to mean that beginners should do green and blue workouts, experienced skaters need to do purple and yellow workouts, and experts should immediately move to orange and red workouts,other options exist. In chapter 13, we will provide you with several programs, arranged into three categories. The appropriate intensity level of your workouts will be determined by not only your experience with in-line skating but also your overall fitness level and your goals.

Within the three categories exist programs designed to provide a smorgasbord of options. You don't need to perform the same workout day in and day out; add some variety. For one week try a few intermediate workouts, followed by an intense workout, then an easy workout; then the next week concentrate on endurance workouts of every intensity.

The programs in chapter 13 are divided into the following three categories:

- **Beginner/easy (Lifestyle):** These workouts are the lowest intensity and are appropriate for individuals with a lower fitness level or those with higher fitness levels who are trying to allow for some active recovery. If your test results from chapter 3 put you in the lower-fitness category, if you simply want to incorporate in-line skating into your life as part of a healthy lifestyle, or if you are relatively new to in-line skating, this category is for you.

- **Frequent/moderate (General Fitness):** If you're interested in skating at least three to four times per week at a moderate level, and in gaining general fitness benefits from exercise, this is the category for you.

- **Competitive/intense (Competition):** The programs outlined in this category are designed to push you to the limit in terms of intensity and duration. If you are contemplating entering a race, or have a serious competitive streak, and you scored high on the time trial in chapter 3, you'll enjoy these programs.

Chapter 12 will help you determine the best way to set up your program by giving you some commonsense tips on how to improve your chances of sticking with your program, as well as outlining three factors that affect the results of training. You'll also learn about training principles that you will need to apply in order to get the most from your workouts. Chapter 13 provides ready-to-go workouts that you can follow based on your goals. Chapter 14 discusses cross-training and how it can help you keep going longer and stronger as you progress in fitness and strength. Finally, chapter 15 describes methods of charting your progress, as well as how to overcome the typical obstacles encountered by would-be prolific exercisers.

12

Setting Up Your Program

First, let's dispel a myth: No pain, no gain. This adage is simply not true for anyone who is new to fitness. It is true, however, that to become a champion racer or Olympic athlete, you'll experience discomfort during training, due mostly to fatigue and stressing the muscles and cardiovascular system to their limits. Most people, though, can obtain tremendous benefits without significant discomfort. As you plan your workouts and training program, plan to take your time building intensity. This helps avoid burnout and overuse injury. Listen to your body. If you feel tired, back off. Don't feel bad about taking it easy for a day or two. Allow your muscles time to rebuild and repair, then get back into your routine.

Unlike some other cardiovascular activities, training with in-line skating is somewhat limited by the available surfaces and the weather. Although some professional racers will skate even in the presence of light rain, we don't recommend that you skate outdoors on wet pavement. When the surface on which you're skating becomes wet, your wheels will slip very easily, which is dangerous. Develop a framework for training that takes into consideration the workout zone you will be using, the weather, and the skating surface. Since you probably have a pretty good idea of what the weather pattern will be like in your area at different times of the year, you can plan your training around climatic conditions. This system of training—one that anticipates problems and allows for solutions—is the most practical way to train.

As you progress in your training, you'll notice workouts that once felt difficult become easier. Try a "next-zone" workout when you're comfortable with the workouts you've mastered. That's part of the fun!

Goal Setting

Consistency is key to reaping the benefits of skate training, and setting goals is one step everyone needs to take to move beyond simply skating for fun (although fun is a valid goal, too). Be realistic as you set goals. If you've been skating for a while and have decided to train for your first 10K, a realistic goal is to select two workouts that push your cardiovascular system at training pace plus one workout devoted to just "going the distance." If you're new to fitness skating, a realistic goal is just to get out there a couple times a week at a low to moderate intensity.

Your personal commitment to exercise will definitely help you move toward reaping the benefits you desire, but sometimes commitment alone isn't enough to make you stick with a training program. If you're going it alone, you're much less likely to continue to exercise. Try the buddy system. Make a pact with another person to meet them on regularly scheduled days each week to skate. Emphasize the fact that your meeting will occur regardless of other commitments; the notion that you have made a promise to meet them will help you and your partner to reach your goal of exercising on a regular basis. Of course, your partner doesn't necessarily have to be skating. For example, a mom wanting to spend more time with her kids (who may be very slow on in-line skates) may want to skate while her kids ride their bicycles. Aside from the camaraderie you can develop, if you skate with another person you'll have someone to talk to, which will make your entire skating experience that much more fun!

Factors Influencing Training Results

You want to get fit using in-line skates, but how do you know where to begin and how hard to work out to achieve your goals? To most effectively reap cardiovascular benefits, it's necessary to consider the three major factors that influence training results:

- Frequency
- Intensity
- Duration

Frequency

Most experts agree that the minimum number of days that you should be active in order to maintain cardiovascular fitness is three per week. For optimum benefits, you should get four to six days per week of exercise. Frequency of exercise is somewhat related to cardiovascular and muscular endurance: the greater the frequency of an activity, the more likely that the endurance (developed principally through increased duration) will be maintained. Increasing exercise frequency without sufficient duration will not significantly improve endurance. When you first start an exercise program of any type, it's prudent to begin slowly (i.e., two to three days per week). As you progress in your confidence, ability to recover, and fitness level, you can increase the frequency to the optimum level of four to six days per week.

Intensity

As mentioned in part II, two methods of measuring intensity—how hard the exercise is relative to your maximal ability—are the rating of perceived exertion (RPE; see table II.1) and percent of maximum heart rate (MHR). RPE is the easier of the two.

The RPE is one of the most user-friendly methods for assessing workout intensity. Because it's based on your personal perception of how hard you're working, there are no equipment requirements, and you can check exercise intensity without stopping (as compared with traditional heart rate checks done without a heart rate monitor). By becoming familiar with the RPE scale, you can ensure a level of exertion that's appropriate to your level of in-line skating fitness and goals for conditioning.

Intensity of exercise is related to muscular strength and number of calories burned; the higher the intensity, the more strength is

© Kevin Syms/F-Stock

The frequency, intensity, and duration of workouts are enhanced by your desire to skate for fun.

required and the greater the number of calories expended. To achieve greater levels of strength and/or expend more calories, you need to increase the intensity of the exercise.

As a beginning in-line skater, you should temper the intensity at which you exercise. Don't expect to gain strength, speed, and power in the first few days or weeks. Start with an intensity that is not too difficult initially. You'll know when you can advance to the next level: when you are able to complete your workouts and your muscles are a bit tired but not sore or aching long after you've finished exercising.

As you make progress, the intensity of your workouts will gradually increase. This intensity increase will result in your needing to take more rest between workouts, in order to allow your muscles to recover completely. For that reason, you won't want to schedule two high-intensity workouts back-to-back. Always schedule at least one low- or moderate-intensity exercise day (if not a total rest day) between high-intensity workout days.

Duration

Duration, or the amount of time spent during an activity, is related to both muscular and cardiovascular endurance, somewhat similar to the frequency of exercise. For optimum results, you should try to skate for at least 30 minutes per session. With increased exercise duration you achieve greater muscular and cardiovascular endurance, but only if a sufficient frequency is also maintained. You cannot expect to maintain your endurance by skating one day per week for four hours, or four days per week for 10 minutes; to achieve optimum benefits you must meet minimum criteria for both duration and frequency.

When initiating your training program, however, it would be wise to keep the duration of your workouts to approximately 30 minutes per session. This will give your muscles, tendons, joints, and cardiorespiratory system a chance to make the adaptations necessary for longer workouts. The workouts in this book progress through 30 minute to 60-minute sessions, and longer. Listen to your body while you make your choices of which workouts you will do next; if you're experiencing undue fatigue or discomfort long after your workouts, you're probably doing too much. If this happens, consider repeating the workouts from either the previous week or the week before, until you feel comfortable and ready to progress.

Training Principles

Now that we've discussed the factors that influence your training, we'll focus on general training principles. One concept that applies to any exercise training program—whether it is a cardiovascular fitness program, a weight training program, or a flexibility program—is that training stresses should have a positive effect. They should maximize benefits and minimize the risk of fatigue or injury. Let's take a look at a few principles that you can use to apply this concept:

- Overload
- Specificity
- Adaptation

Overload

To help assure improvement, workloads must be of a sufficient intensity to impose demands on your muscular and energy systems. If you consistently perform the same activities, your body won't be forced to adapt to meet excess demands above and beyond the load you impose. Therefore, in order to increase any aspect of your fitness (strength, endurance, etc.), you need to perform work at a load beyond that to which you've become accustomed. Likewise, as adaptation to increased loading takes place, more load needs to be added for you to improve. Increasing either the intensity, frequency, or duration of your activities will impose overload to improve at least one aspect of fitness.

Monitoring your heart rate is a good way to check the gains you've made by overload and adaptation to exercise. As fitness levels improve, heart rate decreases. This happens both at rest and at any given workload. The effect is that to maintain a specific heart rate, you have to work harder. Measuring heart rate helps you monitor the progression.

Specificity

The training principle of specificity holds that your training should specifically reflect the biomechanical and physiologic demands of your sport as much as possible. That simply means that if you are going to become a competitive runner, you should run but also perform those activities that mimic the movements and intensity of running. Likewise for in-line skating: if you want to become better at skating, you won't want to spend most of your training time in a swimming pool; the crossover effect is slight.

Difficulties can arise when your cross-training activities involve opposing performance demands. For example, leg strength and endurance developed through cycling transfer easily to Alpine skiing; however, the stop-and-go nature of skiing has a negative effect when transferred to distance endurance riders. If you mix different sports and activities (see chapter 14), your body may lose sport-specific efficiency that is possible only with specific skill rehearsal.

On a more positive note, making unfamiliar skill adaptations may improve your balance in motion. Although most sports don't duplicate the movements of in-line skating very well (the lateral leg

© John Laptad/F-Stock

Use in-line skating workouts to complement movements and skills of your other activities.

motion is unusual), they do provide other benefits, such as strength, endurance, and flexibility. Be aware, though, that strength gains in muscles are relative to the speed and range of motion at which you train. For example, if you train your legs to pedal slowly on a bicycle but you apply a large amount of force, you will gain strength for that movement; however, you will not necessarily be able to transfer that strength to pedaling rapidly. In other words, in order for you to get the most benefit, try to gear your training to movements that mimic the movements of in-line skating.

Adaptation

When a demand is placed on your body, it responds in a specific manner, one result of which is adaptation. Aerobic training produces adaptations in the circulatory, muscular, and nervous systems. By pushing these systems in a progressive pattern, you enhance cardio-vascular and muscle endurance, strength, and flexibility.

The next chapter deals with workouts that are "ready to go"; all you need to do is select your goals and consider your current fitness level.

© Tom McCarthy/Unicorn Stock Photos

Once you understand how to use skates to train, you might be surprised that your goals have shifted—maybe even to include racing.

13

Sample In-Line Skating Programs

Regardless of what activity level you've set as your goal, in-line skating can be incorporated into your lifestyle. Whether you want to use skating as a method to keep yourself active, improve your fitness level, or help you get involved with competition, you'll find a program in this chapter that will help get you there.

As noted earlier, you should have some idea of your fitness level from the skating time trial you performed (chapter 3). Based on both your starting fitness level and your goals, you can select from the three types of training programs outlined in these pages. You may find even the basic-level Lifestyle workouts to be difficult, especially the first time through, but remember that with practice and training, you'll be able to enjoy the effort you put out, as well as the benefits you gain.

Lifestyle Program

If you're not an experienced in-line skater, chances are good that you'll need to take a few weeks (maybe months, depending on your fitness and activity level) to build up your muscles to the point at which you're comfortable doing all of the green and blue zone workouts. Don't worry; even Eddie Matzger (the world-champion speed skater) didn't do his first workout in the red zone. It takes time; if you rush, you may be setting yourself up for injury.

© Larry Pierce/F-Stock

To fit in-line skating into your lifestyle, skate to relax in addition to working out.

Building Endurance

The first Lifestyle-level program focuses on gaining some endurance. These workouts will build your endurance to allow you to skate for at least 30 minutes nonstop without experiencing fatigue. Both of the Lifestyle programs are ideal for partner training; you'll see that the other person is also working, and you can encourage each other to continue.

In the following workouts, colors and numbers represent distinct workouts described in chapters 6 through 11. The moon and window shade symbol indicates a rest day. Remember that the workout zones are graduated in duration, intensity, and distance, beginning with green and moving on to blue, purple, yellow, orange, and red. Also, workouts in most sections progress from easier to harder; for example, green zone workout #1 is easier than green zone workout #2. For example, in the first week's workout schedule, Sunday's workout represents the green zone workout #1 followed by a rest day on Monday.

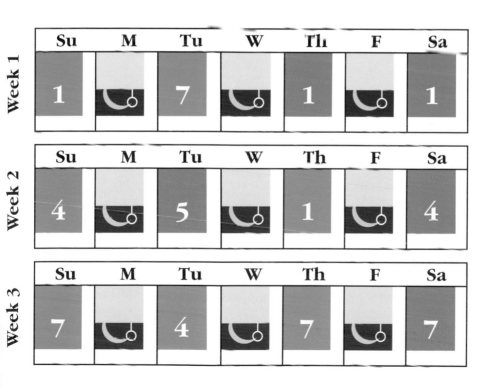

Building Speed

The second Lifestyle-level program focuses more on attaining speed during longer workouts. Although you won't be concentrating on skating fast, you will challenge yourself a bit, which makes the workouts more interesting. Again, if you can get a partner to work with you, you'll have a much easier time maintaining your intensity.

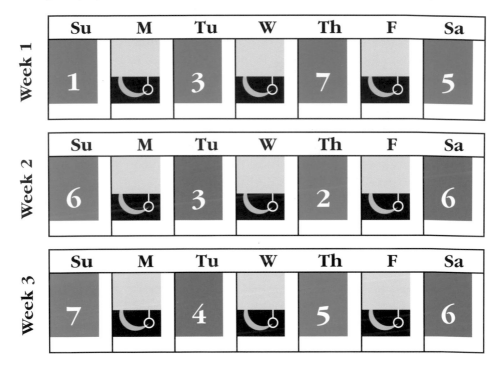

General Fitness Program

If you've chosen the General Fitness program, you're probably already doing some moderate-level activity, so you can expect to do a bit more work than you would by selecting the Lifestyle program schedule. If you're interested in becoming proficient at in-line skating, you'll need to practice, and that's what these workouts are for—they'll keep you on your skates.

Building Endurance

The first General Fitness program focuses on lots of practice. This will translate into lots of miles and lots of time on your skates—just what you'll need to make changes in your performance.

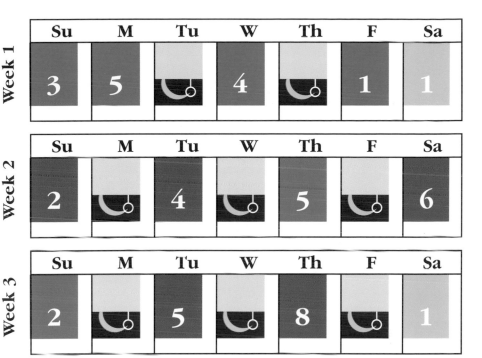

	Su	M	Tu	W	Th	F	Sa
Week 1	3	5	☍	4	☍	1	1
Week 2	2	☍	4	☍	5	☍	6
Week 3	2	☍	5	☍	8	☍	1

Building Speed

The second General Fitness program is geared toward gaining some speed. You should already have some endurance from the first program in this section, or from other training you are doing. These workouts can be somewhat difficult, especially during the last week, when you have three workouts in a row. Stick to it; if you can get through the first two weeks, you can do the final week.

© Gretchen Palmer/F-Stock

Speedplay with a workout partner is an effective way to train.

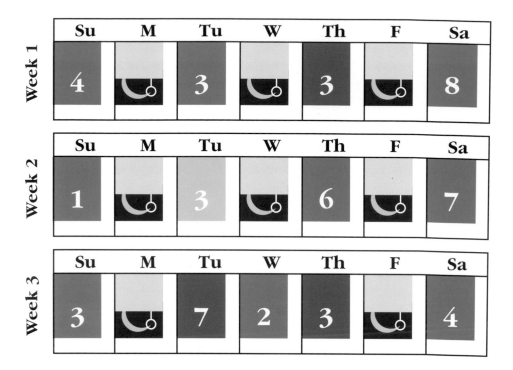

Competition Training Program

The Competition training program is designed specifically for the competitive athlete who wants to get involved with in-line skate racing. If you've chosen this program, you should be able to do a 10K skate race competitively. Although you don't have to follow the suggested workouts exactly as they're presented (since everyone responds differently), you'll get a good idea of how they're laid out so that you can modify them as necessary. Briefly, the workouts are arranged to follow a format that allows for recovery between workouts. Thus, you won't be doing two or three hard workouts in a row; you should intersperse longer-distance, lower-intensity workouts with the higher-intensity sessions.

Building Endurance

The first Competitive-level program will let you know if you're in racing shape or not. If you can't finish the first week, you're not ready for the next two weeks. If that happens, you can simply replace one or two of the workouts with workouts in the green or purple zones.

This will provide you with a few shorter workouts between the longer workouts in this program. If you make it through these workouts, you'll be putting in plenty of time and miles, so get ready. Don't worry if you can't complete these workouts your first time out—it may take some practice.

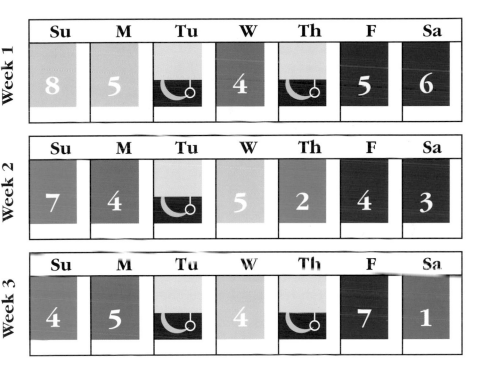

Option: On Thursday of the second week, you can either do the green zone #2 workout or rest, depending on how you feel.

Building Speed

The second Competition-level program focuses on speed—getting you ready for a race. You may need to do a week of this program at a time (i.e., complete week 1, skate at a lower intensity for the next week, complete week 2, skate at a lower intensity for the next week, then complete week 3) if your fitness level isn't high enough to allow you to fully recover between workouts. One good gauge of your recovery between workouts is your resting pulse rate. If your resting pulse rate begins to be higher on successive days, you may be overtraining and need to take it a bit easier.

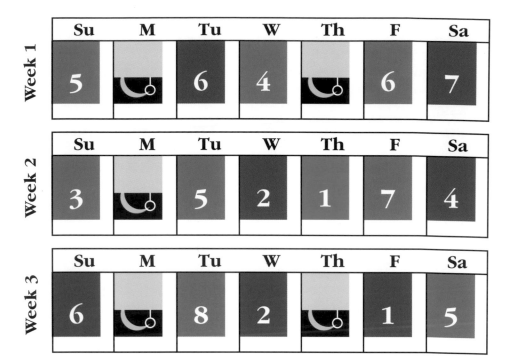

Option: On Thursday of the second week, you can either do the green zone workout #1 or rest, depending on how you feel.

14

Cross-Training

In-line skating, as you can see, is a tremendous activity in many respects, but making it your only fitness activity would be somewhat like making salad your only source of food. Although both in-line skating and salad offer a reasonable amount of value in the diversity and benefits they provide, selecting only one source for physical activity doesn't supply all of the facets necessary for a well-rounded program, just as choosing one source for food won't supply all of the nutritional variety necessary for a well-rounded diet. While in-line skating can be a cornerstone for your exercise program, a popular and almost essential method of assuring a well-rounded exercise program is through the use of cross-training.

Cross-training with various activities is one of the most time-efficient and safe ways to improve your cardiovascular endurance, muscular fitness, muscular endurance, body composition, and flexibility. In addition to the psychological benefits to be gained, cross-training reduces the risk of overuse injury and increases the number of muscles you use, as well as how you use them, which results in a more well-rounded development of your muscles. For example, to cross-train for downhill skiing, you may choose to cross-train with in-line skating for the lateral motions of edging, and cross-train with running to facilitate linear leg movements to absorb irregular terrain-like moguls.

Overuse injuries, which are common in many activities, typically result from using a muscle or body part too much. Repetitive stresses placed on any body part can become overwhelming. If the amount of stress is too much for a muscle, tendon, ligament, or joint to deal with adequately, you'll sustain an injury. Many runners, for example, experience injuries at some point in their careers due to the constant use of specific muscles and to stresses placed on certain joints. Both pulled hamstrings and tendinitis can be related to overuse.

Your body needs rest every day, and so do your muscles and tendons. Performing the same motions without adequate rest can lead to problems. Therefore, in-line skating, although it is a good aerobic activity, should be part of an entire program of exercise. Just as the top Olympic-level athletes in many sports realize the potential for overuse injuries and incorporate rest days, easy days, and cross-training days into their programs, you should also recognize the benefits of cross-training.

Certain sports provide benefits in specific fitness areas. For instance, while cross-training with weight lifting may help your flexibility, muscular strength, and muscular endurance (to a small degree) for in-line skating, weight lifting won't help your cardiovascular endurance or coordination. On the other hand, bicycling will help with muscular strength and endurance, cardiovascular endurance, and, to a lesser extent, coordination, but it will do little to increase the flexibility required for in-line skating.

There is no perfect cross-training activity, but that's the fun part—you get to engage in a variety of activities and reap some of the unique benefit combinations they offer. Table 14.1 categorizes some of the training characteristics specific to in-line skating that are provided by various other sports.

By having more than one sport in your training arsenal, you broaden the number of possible "excellent" ratings in various fitness categories. Mixing and matching the activities in which you participate will enhance not only your ability to engage in a larger variety of activities, but also the benefits that each activity has to offer.

Another benefit of cross-training is the psychological relief it provides; instead of consistently doing the same sport, you can switch activities to help inject a bit of fun and change into your training

Table 14.1
Training Benefits of Various Sports

Activity	Cardiovascular endurance	Muscular strength	Muscular endurance	Flexibility	Coordination
Cycling	Excellent	Good	Very good	Fair	Good
Ice-skating	Good	Very good	Excellent	Very good	Excellent
Rowing	Excellent	Good	Good	Fair	Fair
Running	Excellent	Good	Very good	Fair	Fair
Snow skiing	Good	Very good	Very good	Good	Very good
Snow-skating	Very good	Very good	Very good	Very good	Excellent
Walking	Good	Fair	Good	Fair	Fair
Weight training	Fair	Excellent	Excellent	Good	Fair

program. Many former high school athletes will recall the phenomenon of burnout, which happens when your attitude toward the sport in which you're participating changes from positive to negative or neutral. This familiarity-breeds-contempt sensation is all too frequently the reason that people discontinue their exercise programs.

Since adding a bit of variety to your workout schedule is a good way to keep things fun, you should take advantage of the psychological benefits of cross-training. Bear in mind, however, that not every other activity will provide you with the same exhilaration as in-line skating. If you like exercising outdoors, you might consider cycling, running, or skiing. If you enjoy indoor exercise, indoor rowing or weight training might be a good choice. With experience in a few sessions of each sport that you're contemplating, you'll soon know if that sport is a good option for cross-training.

You can integrate these sports into your training program by using the workouts in this book but substituting the new cross-training sport for in-line skating. For example, workout #4 in the orange zone calls for random-interval training for a total of 35 minutes. If you want to substitute cycling on that day, simply do the intervals on your bicycle. The Comments for that workout will not apply, but the cardiovascular benefits will be very similar.

In order to maximize the benefits of specificity of training, the number of cross-training days per month may be decreased during the peak in-line skating season (especially if you're racing).

Cycling

Bicycling is a good all-around fitness activity as well as a fantastic cross-training tool for in-line skaters. Although the cycling motion does not mimic the in-line skating motion exactly, it is very similar and uses many of the same leg muscles. If you choose cycling for one of your cross-training activities, be sure to get a bike that fits you. Any local bicycle shop with an experienced staff (who are usually cyclists themselves) can help you select a bike to suit your needs and budget. The most popular types of bicycles are versatile; mountain bikes have gained significant favor and are used not only off-road, but for commuting and exercising as well. These wide-tire machines have simple shifting systems and even suspension systems that until recently were found only on motorcycles. For $400 to $700, you can get a good mountain bike that will last for years.

A stationary bicycle offers a suitable alternative for people who don't live in a climate that allows year-round cycling outdoors. Look for a stationary bike with a workload indicator (preferably watts). This feature allows you to accurately reproduce your workload and keep track of your workout intensity. So-called air-resistance bicycles such as the Schwinn Air-Dyne™, which uses vanes attached to the spokes of the bicycle's moving wheel, provide accurate and reproducible workloads.

One worthwhile investment you should consider when using bicycling as a cross-training activity is a pair of padded bicycle shorts. Normal exercise shorts don't have an adequate amount of padding in the seat area to alleviate soreness from sitting on a bicycle saddle for an extended period. Bicycle shorts typically come with a chamois liner in the seat area, which is much more comfortable than the stitched seam found in most exercise shorts. In addition, cycling shorts are made with a stretchable material that conforms to your legs, reducing the friction and rubbing against the bicycle seat that you might experience with other shorts. Bicycle shorts shouldn't be confused with padded in-line skating shorts; skating shorts have impact-reducing foam pads on the hips and tailbone, while cycling shorts use friction-reducing padding in only

© John Plummer/F-Stock

Take to the roads on a bike for a change of pace.

the seat area of the pants. Cycling shorts are worth the $30 to $70 investment.

Two other convenient, comfortable items should complete your cycling equipment needs: gloves and shoes. Padded gloves make cycling more comfortable on the palms of the hands, while cycling shoes are constructed with a rigid sole to make pedaling more efficient.

Ice-Skating

Ice-skating is a very good crossover sport for in-line skaters. Although many ice-skaters who've tried in-line skating say that it's much easier in terms of balance, ice-skating movements mimic in-line movements quite well. One of the major drawbacks of ice-skating, however, is the necessity of an ice surface on which to practice.

If you are fortunate enough to have access to an ice surface for skating, consider the benefits of cross-training with ice-skating. The lateral leg motion movements of in-line skating are almost duplicated with ice-skating, the balance and coordination required for ice-skating help with in-line skating balance, and you will feel as though you don't need to concentrate nearly as much while in-line skating as you do while ice-skating, due to the small surface on which you're placing all of your weight while ice-skating.

Unfortunately, due to the lack of exposure and popularity of ice-skating, the selection of ice skates at sports shops is more limited than your choice of in-line skates. If you're purchasing ice skates, make sure you speak with a knowledgeable salesperson in order to find a pair that will help you in your cross-training.

Rowing

Rowing outdoors may be a good way to get your exercise, but many people don't have ready access to a waterway. The good news is that indoor rowing has become a tremendously popular activity in the past 10 years with the advent of the indoor rowing ergometer. In fact, competitions are regularly held around the world using indoor rowing machines. The upper-body muscular strength development, along with the cardiovascular gains that are possible with this sport, make it a top choice for keeping your workouts well rounded and balanced.

Since in-line skating primarily develops the muscles of the legs, many people don't see the utility of also exercising the upper body. However, a closer look at the motions used to sprint, climb, or even start moving on in-line skates reveals that the upper body can be a strong factor in your ability to perform well and comfortably. If all other factors are equal between two skaters, the skater with the stronger upper body will win in a sprint—it's that simple. Even if you're not interested in sprinting or racing, rowing provides a method of achieving upper-body development that will help you in all of your normal, non-sports-related daily activities.

Most people remember the old-fashioned rowing machine, which resembled a short chair with two shock absorbers attached to the rowing arms. The new rowing ergometer of choice for many international competitors is the Concept II™, a flywheel-driven rower that displays how much work you've done, how many calories you've burned, and how far you've rowed (based on the work you've done). You can seek out a good rower at your local fitness club or YMCA; if you prefer to purchase one, expect to pay about $750. Remember, though, that nothing else will exercise your upper body and provide for total body development aerobically like a rowing ergometer. When incorporated into an in-line skating program, it truly makes an all-around training program.

Running

Running doesn't require a lot of equipment and provides significant cardiovascular benefits. However, a major drawback is the high-impact nature of the activity. Because of that, heavier people and those with previous orthopedic problems should probably consider a different cross-training activity.

For the rest of the population, the major benefits of running that cross over to in-line skating are muscular and cardiovascular endurance. Even though the muscles employed in running are not used in the same way that they are used during in-line skating, adding a program of running to your in-line training program can lend some versatility and improve your endurance. Be aware, though, that you should not increase your running mileage more than about 10 percent per week, to reduce the risk of overuse injury. A good pair of running shoes can cost anywhere from $60 to $150.

Snow-Skating

The rapidly growing sport of snow-skating is often a welcome diversion for in-line skaters. Snow skates are lightweight, supportive boots with a replaceable base that allow participants to glide across the snow as if in-line skating or ice-skating. Just watching someone snow-skate downhill and across level snow-covered ground tells the story about the benefits; the movements are almost a winter's mirror image of in-line skating movements.

Many of the muscle groups used in snow-skating are also exercised during in-line skating, making it a highly advantageous off-season sport for in-line skaters. Likewise, the skills that you develop while in-line skating transfer to this activity.

Aside from the obvious muscular strength benefits of this activity due to the specificity-of-training principle, you can also develop muscular endurance, flexibility, and coordination. Snow-skating is one of the few activities that allow you to continue your in-line skating technique practice year-round, regardless of the weather. Snow skates are available for less than $200 for beginner- to intermediate-level skates and less than $300 for elite-level skates. If you're interested in trying snow-skating, look for rentals available at many ski areas for approximately $8 to $15 a day. (Although the falls are much less impactful than on in-line skates, since you're landing on snow, wearing wrist guards is a good precaution the first time you're on snow skates.)

Courtesy of The Sled Dogs Co./Skater: Dave Desrochers

Snow-skating is an excellent cross-training activity for the winter months.

Snow Skiing and Snow-Boarding

Alpine (downhill) skiing has many benefits to in-line skaters, including a very accurate transfer of similar skills. The movement and skills involved turning downhill on in-line skates are almost identical to those movements and skills required to turn downhill on skis. Acquiring balance and coordination are added benefits. In addition, snow skiing requires strength in the quadriceps, making it an ideal cross-training activity for development or maintenance of leg strength throughout the year.

Alpine snow skiing requires cardiovascular endurance, muscular endurance, flexibility, and coordination, all of which also benefit in-line skaters. One possibly negative feature of Alpine skiing is that you need to have access to a ski lodge or other snow-covered area with a system of transportation to the top. Snow skis can be rented at most

Snow skiing also provides cross-training benefits for in-line skaters.

ski lodges for approximately $15 to $20 per day, and prices for buying a beginner package start as low as $350.

Snow-boarding is another snow sport that requires coordination, flexibility, and muscular endurance. A snowboard resembles a skateboard but with a longer base and no wheels. Bindings mounted on top of the snowboard allow users to attach themselves securely for maneuverability and control.

Since your feet are not parallel with your line of travel while on a snowboard (they're placed diagonally and, in some cases, perpendicular to the line of travel), the leg and ankle motion is unlike that encountered while in-line skating. On the other hand, the total body control requirements of snow-boarding make it a good balancing activity. Snowboards are available for rental at some ski areas for approximately $20 to $30 per day, while the cost of a new board starts at $250.

Weight Training

Most athletes use weight training to supplement their other training, even on the days when they practice their major sport. While this might sound like a good way to maximize your time, remember that if your muscles are fatigued from weight training, they may not be able to perform well in your activity. Likewise, if you do your activity first, you might be too fatigued to get any significant benefits from weight training on the same day.

Weight training is a broad term that can include anything from training with free weights (dumbbells and barbells), to machines that have weight stacks, to hydraulic or pneumatic-driven machines, to machines with cam-type systems that are designed to increase the resistance you encounter as you go through a movement. Any of this equipment can yield benefits for in-line skating, if used correctly. The key is to be consistent. Using resistance training regularly is more beneficial than using it once per month. Starting your resistance training program early (a few months before you plan on skating) will help prepare you for the challenges you'll face. Start your resistance training program by lifting two to three days per week for at least four to six weeks.

The principal considerations when initiating a weight training program are the following:

- **Muscles to be trained:** Typically, you will want to focus on the quadriceps, hamstrings, adductors (inner thigh) and abductors (outer thigh), calves, shins, gluteals, lower back, abdomen, hip flexors, upper arms, upper back, chest, and shoulders for a well-rounded yet manageable program.
- **Speed of movement:** Pay attention to how much time you spend in the "work" phase of the lift. If you're using anything except a pneumatically controlled machine, you should perform the movement in a controlled, slow manner. Some pneumatically controlled machines allow you to maintain a set resistance regardless of the speed of the movement.
- **Amount of lifting:** You should begin with two to three sets of 10 to 15 repetitions of each exercise. Once you've attained your goals, you can maintain your strength by continuing to lift at least once per week, but no more than three times per week (with at least one rest day between resistance training sessions).

Putting It All Together

All of the cross-training possibilities presented in this chapter are great for in-line skaters; each offers a different set of benefits. You can choose one, two, or all of them. One of the nicest things about cross-training is that you can do it whenever the mood hits you—and you can just "play" with your workouts and still enjoy benefits. Remember that you can always intersperse a variety of activities into your training program by simply replacing in-line skating with the activity of your choice at least once a week.

15

Charting Your Progress

Make no mistake about it: continuing an exercise program holds many challenges, but with a bit of understanding about what conditions tend to cause people to quit their exercise regimens, you can plan ahead to help stay on track. No matter which of the following suggestions you employ in your quest for fitness and better health, you should combine them with keeping a journal of your exercise program.

The major reason most people cite for discontinuing an exercise program is lack of time. However, if you examine what you do during a typical day, you may be surprised to find that you spend at least a small amount of time engaged in nonproductive activities such as watching television, talking on the phone, or just sitting around bored. If you plan ahead, you'll find you can do a workout at some time during the day, at least three or four days every week.

Lack of planning is another inhibitor to staying with an exercise program. If you don't schedule a time to do your skating (or other exercise), chances are that something else will come up to keep you from doing the activity. On the other hand, if you make specific plans to do your skating at the same time every day or every other day, you're more likely to continue. Scheduling exercise for certain days of the week is a good method of ensuring consistency. For instance, if you schedule your workouts for Monday, Wednesday, and Friday evenings at five o'clock, you're much more likely to follow through than if you simply say, "I'll get to it when I have time." Writing your schedule on a calendar also helps increase the chance that you'll exercise. If it's scheduled, it's more likely to get done (especially if it's scheduled with a buddy). Call a friend and make an appointment to skate every Monday, Wednesday, and Friday. Go to a skating rink on Tuesday and Thursday. Tell a coworker that you want to make it a date to skate three days per week—his or her choice. Putting any of these ideas into practice will make you more likely to be consistent.

Another motivational trick is to have a goal in mind. It may be as specific as finishing the upcoming 10K skate race in under 28 minutes, or as broad as competing in a 10K race by November. Either way, you have some idea where you're headed. If you don't know where you're going, how will you know when you get there? You can keep your goal written on the top page of your exercise journal; that way you're able to see what you're working toward every time you make an entry.

Create a Training Journal

In order to really derive the benefits of training, you must continue to train and identify the elements that make training difficult and less productive for you. Since every person responds differently to the same training regimen, you should keep track of how you feel after each workout, so that you can recognize and correct problems if they occur. For example, you may be very good at recovering from intense workouts twice a week but unable to make it on longer workouts. For you, depending on your goals, becoming a good endurance skater may not even be necessary. If your goal is to skate shorter distances more intensely, you might do fine by continuing your current training program. If, on the other hand, you want to be able to skate longer distances, maybe you should change your workouts to include more long, slow distance and back off on the intense workouts.

© Jane Dove Juneau

Noting how you feel after your workout is as important as recording your workout in a training journal.

A training journal provides clues as to which workouts produce the most results, as well as which ones make you the most tired. While most journals contain only basic workout information such as time and distance skated, others include more precise details such as resting heart rate before and after the workout, RPE, distance, speed, terrain, temperature, wind conditions, and unusual factors such as traffic stops or water breaks.

As we mentioned, your journal can be as simple or as complex as you prefer. An example of a simple workout journal in calendar form follows.

			Training Log			
Sunday	Monday	Tuesday	Wednesday	Thursday	Friday	Saturday
			Skate green 2 great		Skate blue 1 great	Bike 25:00 legs tired
	Skate green 4 great	Walk 45:00 easy		Skate green 1 windy		
Skate green 3 easy		Skate blue 2 easy	Walk 50:00 easy		Skate blue 1 great	
Bike 40:00 hard		Skate green 4 so-so		Skate green 3 easy		Walk 45:00 easy
	Skate blue 2 great		Skate blue 3 great		Row 25:00 hard	

A quick glance tells you how many days per week you exercised, what activity you performed, how you felt during each workout, and even what in-line skating workouts you did (using the respective workout number from chapters 6 through 11).

Variables that some athletes find useful in their journals include resting heart rate upon waking and before working out, recovery heart rate (1 minute, 2 minutes, 5 minutes, 10 minutes, and 30 minutes after a workout), body weight, time of day, outdoor temperature, humidity/wind conditions, RPE, as well as general feelings regarding workout (felt great, very hard, difficult to concentrate, tired, etc.).

Here is an example of a more detailed exercise log for in-line skaters.

Training Log	
Date:	Wed., July 9
Resting heart rate (A.M.):	64
Workout time:	4:30 P.M. begin; total workout: 44:28
Temperature/conditions:	67 degrees, calm wind, few rolling hills
Course location:	Rouge Park
Workout description:	20K Race Pace
Resting heart rate (preworkout):	72
Total workout distance:	20K (12.4 miles)
Exercise heart rate(s):	average: 158
Exercise RPE:	8 or 9
Recovery heart rates:	1 min: 132; 2 min: 114; 5 min: 90; 10 min: 84; 30 min: 76
Comments/rating:	Felt good during first half of workout; drank two full water bottles of water

Depending on your goals, you can glean a lot of useful information from the facts that you record in your training journal. For example, a significant decrease in body weight combined with high outdoor temperatures and higher resting heart rates may indicate that you're becoming either dehydrated or overtrained from working too hard. Conversely, if you constantly feel great after workouts, you may be able to increase the intensity or duration, perhaps even moving to the next workout zone. Whatever method you choose, simple or more detailed, you'll be able to look back at your training journals for years and see how much fun you had with in-line skating.

Reward Yourself

Whenever you start a new project, sport, or task of any sort, your motivation to continue depends in part on your perception of your progress. One easy way to help ensure your continued participation with in-line skating is to set up a schedule of rewards. This can mean anything from writing on a slip of paper, "I will treat myself to a movie if I finish three continuous weeks of three-times-per-week in-line skating," to promising to buy yourself a new set of in-line skate wheels after you accumulate 300 miles on your skates. Take a few minutes to jot down some ideas for your own reward system as soon as you finish this chapter. That will give you a head start on your plan to skate consistently. Keep in mind that the best reward is how good you feel at the end of each workout!

You're On Your Own!

We've given you everything you need in order to use in-line skates successfully to become and stay fit. What we can't provide is the constant motivation to stick with it; that part is up to you. Remember that in order to optimize the benefits and enjoyment offered by in-line skating, you need to do it consistently. Every minute of every day, you have another chance to make the right choices for a healthier lifestyle. We hope those choices will include working out consistently on in-line skates!

A final thought: Once you've reached a point in your in-line skating workouts that you've pretty much done it all, our bet is that you'll come to enjoy the value of simply skating for peace of mind; the benefits reaped from in-line skating can be as good for your head as they are for your body. We wish you the best of luck. And—who knows—maybe we'll see you out there skating sometime!

© Caroline Wood/F-Stock

Now it's up to you. Be a fitness in-line skating ambassador; recruit your friends!

Index

Note: Page references to photographic illustrations are italicized.

About
the Authors

Suzanne Nottingham is one of the nation's leading skating instructors. By working with the International In-Line Skating Association and coauthoring the IISA Level 1 Fitness Certification Manual, she led the effort to merge the fitness and in-line skating industries. Her background includes 17 years as a ski instructor at Mammoth Mountain, California, and 5 years as the fitness advisor to Rollerblade.

Nottingham lives in Mammoth Lakes, California, with her husband Peter, daughter Taylor, and son Lucas. In addition to winter sports, they enjoy in-line skating, mountain biking, hiking, and gardening.

Frank J. Fedel is an exercise specialist and researcher at the Henry Ford Heart and Vascular Institute in Dearborn Heights, Michigan. He conducted the first research study to examine the cardiovascular responses of competitive in-line skaters during skating. In addition to having a scientific focus, Fedel himself has been a very successful competitive in-line skater since 1991. He is a member of the American College of Sports Medicine.

Frank Fedel lives in Royal Oak, Michigan, with his wife, Helen, who is also a competitive in-line racer. He enjoys cycling, mountain biking, and weight training in addition to in-line skating.

Look for these other titles in the Fitness Spectrum Series

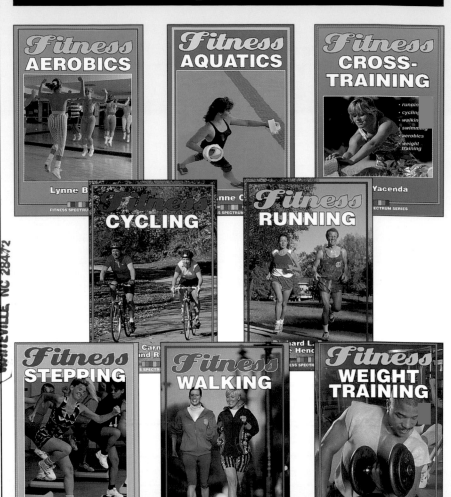

Forthcoming Titles:
Fitness Swimming
Fitness Cross-Country Skiing

Human Kinetics
http://www.humankinetics.com/

2335

To place your order, U.S. customers
call TOLL FREE 1 800 747-4457.
Customers outside the U.S. place your
order using the appropriate
telephone number/address shown
in the front of this book.